# FROM GLASGOW
# TO THE ANDES

# FROM GLASGOW TO THE ANDES

*by*
Blanquita Haggerty

RITCHIE

John Ritchie Publishing

40 Beansburn, Kilmarnock, Scotland

ISBN-13: 978 1 914273 04 9


Copyright © 2021 by John Ritchie Ltd.
40 Beansburn, Kilmarnock, Scotland


www.ritchiechristianmedia.co.uk

Typeset by John Ritchie Ltd., Kilmarnock
Printed by Bell & Bain Ltd., Glasgow

*The Haggerty Family*

FROM GLASGOW TO THE ANDES

FROM GLASGOW TO THE ANDES

# CONTENTS

# PREFACE

Missionary biographies are usually highly readable and interesting. This one is no exception. Vivid, lively, and entertaining as it is, one might forget that there are lessons in it for all who know the Saviour. Two struck me as I read.

First, it is surely the case that the teenage Frank Haggerty would have seemed to most of us as very unlikely material for a missionary. Raised in a poor part of Glasgow as a Roman Catholic. Active as a gang member and gang leader. He was more likely to follow one of his companions to execution in Barlinnie jail than to set sail for Bolivia to preach the Gospel! Yet Frank, reflecting on his early life, saw that God was preparing him, even before his conversion, for his subsequent service. This is illustrated well in the book. Dealing with issues on the mission field, he was greatly helped by his early experiences. It is a reminder that God is the potter, we are the clay. He moulds us after His plan and for His purpose.

The second lesson came from the story of Frank's salvation. With no real knowledge of God or of the Gospel, he started work in a Glasgow factory. There, another young man took note of him, showed kindness to him, explained the way of salvation to him and continued to influence Frank's growth as a Christian. That person was Harry Burness who later became a well-known and highly respected evangelist. Frank's testimony shows that Harry took the opportunity given to him to be God's instrument in reaching out to Frank. How many opportunities we miss! Little did Harry realize just how important his interest in Frank would be for the work of God in Bolivia. The personal witness of a Christian to a fellow-worker can have consequences beyond any expectation.

Enjoy the book and see what else you might learn from this absorbing account of a life given to the Lord.

W. Stevely

# PROLOGUE: FROM GLASGOW TO THE ANDES

This book by Blanquita Haggerty, my Mum, tells the story of her beloved Frank, Dad. It begins with Frank in Scotland, then tells how each of them came to their vocation as missionaries, how they formed a unique and effective team. The focus is on the early formative years of their joint calling that set the foundation for their eventual rooting and fruitfulness in Santa Cruz, Bolivia.

This book starts off, somewhat surprisingly in Frank's voice. This is because Frank Haggerty was a gifted story teller who crafted his stories carefully, orchestrated their telling with tone and gesture that engaged the audience as he set the scene, built the tension to a climax, and brought finally a satisfying resolution. As I read Mum's retelling of this story, I hear Dad's voice. One of our family joys was sitting at the table after supper, completely enthralled and engaged in one of Dad's stories. It could be about Scottish history or the life of Jesus or memories of his childhood. It did not matter that we might have heard the story many times. In church, it would be a great treat when Dad would tell a Bible story in an all-ages church service. He would test audience engagement by stopping to ask what happened next, or making an obvious mistake and the audience would roar their correction to the wrong turn that Dad had taken in the story or would fill in the blanks. Much of this book is informed by Dad's stories.

But this is Blanquita's story. Mum was a very different kind of story teller. Her stories echo her Spanish culture of story-telling in the afternoon café or accompanying the needlework around a common source of light. The style was more rambling and musing, built around juicy titbits. The unwary listener could find oneself hurled without warning to another time or space, or encounter a character appearing out of nowhere. It was the context of the larger story or the moral – often discerned in retrospect – that brought coherence and satisfaction to the story. *In this telling of Frank and Blanquita's story, these musings are indicated in italics.*

*Blanquita Haggerty*

But mostly, this book is a love letter written by Blanquita Haggerty.

In this story, foreign missionaries figure large. Some missionaries became their best friends and support in what could be a lonely leadership position. In part, this is a love letter to them. But in writing this book, Blanquita must also have had in mind the audience "at home" – those faithful supporters whose prayers and giving made the missionary life possible. Mum spent a lot of time writing to people to thank them for their gifts and tell them about their work. This is her final letter to them, a love letter.

The book is also a love letter to her grandchildren, and especially to her grandsons who were young men when she started this book. She told me that she wanted them to know their Papa, not as the old man of their memory, but as the young courageous man who was their age when she first knew him. She wanted them to know him and love him, out of time as it were. She hoped that they would recognize in themselves some of his spiritual and visionary legacy to them. When their Papa understood God's love for him in Jesus, his life was totally transformed. How she longed for her beloved grandchildren to meet Jesus and experience that transformation and greater purpose!

Finally, and of course, it is a love letter written by Blanquita Haggerty (née Weise Montero) for Frank Haggerty, about Frank and their life together. Where Dad was the dreamer and adventurer, Mum was the pragmatist and planner. Where Dad was rough and ready, Mum was elegant and poised. They were an amazing team. Mum started writing this book in 2014 as she emerged from mourning Dad's death in 2003. The book gave her a new purpose in her later years.

13

I am so grateful to The Lord's Work Trust and to John Ritchie Publishing for seeing the value of this book. Their endorsement was such a gift to Blanquita, and it is a gift to our family to have this record. She wrote this book as she was losing her sight from macular degeneration. My thanks to Bill Stevely, who did the first round of editing, and to Fraser Munro for final polishing. It has been my privilege to finish editing it for my Mum. I tried to preserve her unique voice (try to imagine it in a Scottish-Spanish accent!), and provide a little context when needed.

Jeannie Haggerty,
September 2021

## Chapter 1

# A GLASGOW BOY

### The Initiation

"The train's coming! The train is nearly here ... Hurry up!"

I heard the shout of the fellows around me ... Yes, the train was coming ... Coming closer and closer!

One could feel the rumble of the train wheels on the sleepers of the railroad track!

With eyes almost popping out of their sockets, the guys were watching me. I could see their excitement and devilry, mixed with signs of doubt. I looked at the expectant faces and could almost read their thoughts ... Is he going to do it? Will he chicken out ... ?

Seeing the smirks on their faces made me more determined to follow the course of action as planned. Liam had given me clear instructions as to what to do and how to do it. In those timeless seconds, I reviewed everything in my mind with crystal clarity.

A while back my brother Liam had been sent to a Borstal School (Correctional Centre). He had achieved the notorious reputation of continually getting into hot water with the police and with the neighbours. The Juvenile Court had finally taken the unpleasant decision to send him away for an enforced vacation at the Government's expense!

Until that time, Liam had been the leader of the gang in our district. His going away would leave the position vacant and the new leader had to prove himself worthy of the position, not only by being tall, or having good fists for street fights, but there was a final thorny test before admittance to the role. The position was open. I was hoping to become the leader by being a good fighter, and able to hold my own, but I still had to go through the initiation, if I was to be held worthy to become the leader.

Partick was a district for working class people in the city of Glasgow. Young fellows at an early age joined gang groups, as a way of protection from groups from other districts. There were Protestant gangs, Roman Catholic gangs, gangs who just wanted to control their streets. The fights were bitter among them, especially when in the name of religion.

Gang groups would come from across the Clyde River to our Partick district, also from other areas of the city. They used to come to pester the neighbourhood girls, create fights in the dance halls, and were not afraid to beat the unwary young fellows they met in the streets. So, to protect our rights to our district we were forced to join a gang at the earliest possible age.

During the years of the Great Depression, parents had to work long hours in order to be able to put bread on the table, so the young ones were left without supervision at home. Such was the case in our home. Mother had passed away when we were quite young and Father brought us up alone. Having to go out to work for our daily sustenance meant we were left in the care of neighbours in the tenement building. We grew quite wise to the time schedule and as soon as Father was due to return home, we were the best behaved boys in the place, so my father could hardly believe the reports of neighbours and police about our misdeeds.

My father, William Haggerty, had been quite a wild fellow in his own youth. He was orphaned young and very much given to adventure. Still quite young he ran away from his arthritic grandmother and slipped aboard a ship, hoping to end up in Australia. He was quite disappointed when he was found and put ashore in Ireland where he stayed for some time until he returned to Scotland.

Some time later, he went to visit a friend at the Western Infirmary in Glasgow. However, finding an empty bed, he was told that his friend had been discharged earlier. His informant was a very nice Irish nurse, Ruby. William was disappointed to miss his friend. What to do with the chocolate box? What better than to give them to the nice Irish nurse ... ? So Ruby became the recipient of the sweets and this was the beginning of the romance which continued into marriage. In due course, three boys were added to the family, Liam, Frank and Jack. A happy family.

However, one day Ruby needed to go into the Western Infirmary for some medical attention. Sadly, my mother Ruby never returned leaving us, the three boys, at a tender age. My father turned to binge drinking out of desperation caused by heartache and depression after his beloved wife died. However, he soon realized he needed to change his way of life in order to look after the three motherless boys. He found refuge in the Church and became a fervent Roman Catholic. He was well known for his care for others in the parish. He decided to bring up his boys by himself as a token of love to his departed wife. He put in every effort possible to impart to us a respect and love for God and the Church. Sad to say, in spite of his good example and teaching, we were always getting into trouble. My father never remarried ... and he could not bring himself to talk to us about our mother of whom we knew hardly anything on account of our tender age when she died.

Near Partickbridge Street there was a railway line and we used to stand near to watch the wagons go by. Sometimes it would be a passenger train, other times it would be freight wagons. We knew the train schedule pretty well from our roaming around the area. But we had to be continually on the lookout for the police as they were out to catch gang boys in their pranks. This was the place to test our mettle to decide who would become the gang leader.

Liam had been very specific about how to go about it. "Remember," he said, "there is a stream of hot water that comes out of the boiler ... Make sure to avoid it or you could get badly scalded ... Remember also that you mustn't show fear or hesitation, because the fellows will be watching you ... Lie facing the sky, only cowards lie facing the ground."

With those words ringing in my ears, I told the gang, "I am ready". With expectant faces they watched me avidly, and when the train was near enough, I jumped onto the sleepers, positioned myself on my back as instructed and waited ... I lay down as flat as possible, my only wish was that I had managed to avoid the runnel of hot water! The reason for waiting until the last moment before jumping in was to avoid giving the engine driver a chance to stop the train prematurely!

And that is how Frank Haggerty became the leader of the "Ten Tom Cats Gang" in the district of Partick! Big brother Liam and little brother Jack were very proud of their middle brother.

This experience was burnt in my brain. I never forgot the feeling of danger, the thundering of the train over me, how the sleepers shook up and down, threatening to throw me up toward the undercarriage of the wagons that were rushing over me. At the time I was too young to fully understand the risks involved in the experience. One thing was clear, this initiation served to strengthen my character in the process of growing.

*(Many, many years later, Frank used to join Eugene (Gene) Train in evangelistic horseback trips in the "Cordillera" mountains in Bolivia. The horseback party would have about six persons on horses and supplies were carried on pack mules. They would go riding all day through canyons, and creeks, crossing rivers, visiting isolated villages and hamlets, sometimes arriving at farms where they would give out tracts and speak to the people about the Gospel of the Good News of Salvation.*

*As a rule, people were glad of visitors to relieve the isolation of their humble surroundings and often in spite of much poverty they would offer welcome and a little refreshment, giving Frank a chance to speak to them about the Lord. They traded New Testaments and portions of Scriptures for food or eggs. It was a good way to place the Word of God into the hands of people. Very early they learned that people who paid something in exchange for Scripture portions would value it, whether it was one or two eggs for a New Testament, but it was something they had acquired at a cost. What a bargain!*

*During one of those trips they had been going since early morning and as night was falling, they arrived at a village. Unlike many villages,* the people were quite unfriendly and would not offer any hospitality. Apparently, there was a wedding celebration and all the villagers were enjoying the occasion which was accompanied by abundant alcoholic libations.

Since they could not get anyone to receive them in their home, they tethered the horses, opened their bedrolls and stretched out under the stars, hoping to get some rest before continuing the next morning to other places. Sleep was hard to come by in spite of their tiredness, because of the noisy celebrations.

Well after midnight the revellers decided to enhance their night enjoyment with a new sport and saddled their horses heading to where the party was lying in the open. With shouts of glee, they started jumping over them showing off their skill with their horses. They were glued to the ground wondering when the dangerous hoofs would land crippling or killing someone.

Thankfully, seeing their lack of response, after a while they tired of the game and went back to their own celebrations. During all that tense time, Frank's memory went back to the experience of lying under the train and that terrifying time was brought back vividly to his memory. That initiation test had not only been a test for a new gang leader, but also a preparation for such times of danger.)

*Chapter 2*

# SEARCHING

Frank had a deep spiritual thirst in his soul in spite of his gang activities. A profound desire to find peace with God led him to become an altar boy in the Roman Catholic Church. He went through all the sacraments of the Church in his search for peace. His father encouraged this inclination in his son since he had found a measure of spiritual help in Church exercises.

Mr. Haggerty sent the three boys to St. Peter's Roman Catholic School in the hope that they would learn good morals and become good citizens.

Frank was not a good student, and was always in conflict with certain teachers. There was one in particular who got fed up with his pranks and yelled at him: "Haggerty, you are heading for the gallows!" However, he moved into the classroom of a Mr. Renuccie, who managed to get to the good side of the student and instilled in him a desire to get good grades and so he became an excellent pupil. As he finished the school, he was offered a grant to go on to higher academic levels. He was elated and told his Dad about this. Unfortunately, Mr. Haggerty had to explain to him that they had no means to pay for the extra expenses like transport and uniforms required in that level of school. Standard school leaving was at the age of fourteen. One could leave school and go to work, or into some type of apprenticeship.

It saddened Frank to miss the opportunity to continue his studies but his brain had already been fired with a thirst for learning avidly from whatever came within his range.

Frank had to find a job as his income was needed to keep the family in the little room and kitchen in Partickbridge Street. After holding different jobs, messenger boy, milk delivery, etc., the Second World War came along and it was easy to find employment. Men and women went out to work, many more enlisted and there were plenty of opportunities. He was still under age, but being a tall fellow appeared older and managed to get a full-time position. It was not unusual for young fellows to lie about their age to get work or to enlist in the army. Liam, the older brother, enlisted quite early and went to war when he was still under age. Jack followed his brother's example and enlisted in the army as well.

Due to Frank's activities as leader in the gang, he had acquired a vile tongue which was very useful to keep his gang companions subdued, and was also very useful for putting fear in the hearts of raiding parties from rival gangs that came into Partick district. He never went in for drinking or smoking since he thought drunkenness reduced men to babbling idiocy. At that time the drug culture hadn't yet appeared.

Frank would often go to Roman Catholic spiritual retreats searching for peace with God. He also went to special retreats of silence to try to cleanse his vile mouth. This was encouraged by his father who found this habit very distasteful. Unfortunately, it never helped because as soon as Frank came home the swear words were back in his mouth. Talk about despair! Both father and son felt disillusioned to find out that all their efforts were useless to change the habit. How often people make resolutions to change things in their lives only to find they don't have the inner strength to carry out the desired changes.

In reality, a person needs to experience a drastic change, akin to a rebirth, in order to be able to change the habits of a lifetime.

Frank had yet to come to know that he needed help from outside himself in order to find the spiritual peace he was looking for, and to find the power to overcome the bad language that came to his lips constantly.

The three Haggerty boys were sent to St. Peter's Catholic School where they were drilled in the Roman Catholic faith. Interesting enough, in school they learned history as taught from the Catholic point of view. Later, Frank found that point of view to be quite at odds with mainstream history. It took him quite a while to accept the correct versions of a number of events in British history!

Frank was about 14/15 years old when he found a job in a factory that was turning out war supplies. Being the youngest in the work force  he was the "gofer" boy for everybody. He especially enjoyed doing errands for the men, though it meant jumping over the wall of the factory, going for cigarettes, or anything they wanted  from outside. There was always a tip of a few pennies.

As the War progressed, changes came to the factory. He was moved to a different section in which women worked at the machines. Being brought up in a home without women he didn't know how to behave with them, and the situation was quite baffling to the young fellow! Women don't send for the things men want. All they wanted was their cup of tea which he would have to bring. No tips were ever given! Poor Frank, he felt he was cheated of his livelihood! Tips were his to keep, but wages went to the home kitty.

Not long after, a new supervisor arrived in the factory, and he was assigned to supervise the women's section, Frank's section. The new supervisor, Harry Burness, was a committed Christian who showed in every way his Christian character. Harry befriended Frank who was the only other male in the section. With spiritual perception he realized that beneath the tough exterior of this young gang leader, there was a heart that had a tremendous desire to know God and experience peace and the forgiveness of sin.

Harry had to be very tactful in speaking to Frank because the young fellow immediately stated his own position according to the Roman Catholic doctrines he had learned. He would not accept anything different. They would discuss themes like the adoration of the Virgin Mary, the apostle Peter as the Pope of Rome and papal succession, along with many other subjects. Frank allowed Harry to see his spiritual thirst, but would not budge from his beliefs.

Harry used to bring some home baking in his lunch bag and often shared with Frank a piece of apple pie or some good baking that came from the hands of Gena, his wife. It is easy to imagine what a treat it was to taste those good things, especially to a young fellow who had grown up without a mother in the home. Sharing a piece of cake or pie broke down the barriers and Frank sensed the goodness that emanated from Harry's heart toward him.

One day, Harry offered Frank a New Testament, challenging him to read the account of the Lord Jesus as presented in the four Gospels. Frank took it home, read it from cover to cover, and was quite confused when he could not find certain narratives in the Gospels, such as the story of the Veil of St. Veronica and others learned in his growing years at St. Peter's School, taught as though they were from the Holy Scriptures.

He didn't find much about the apostle Peter either, and nothing about his ordination as the first Pope. In fact, a number of other practices which had been drilled into him as "practices given in the Holy Scriptures" were non-existent in the New Testament.

*Chapter 3*

# FINDING

After reading the New Testament, Frank went back to Harry with many of questions. This allowed Harry to speak more clearly about the love of God. He told Frank how the Lord Jesus Christ came to save sinners and how He gave Himself as a sacrifice for sinners who need to repent of their sin and accept the offer of forgiveness by God. It was very confusing for Frank to realise that, apart from the Lord Jesus, there was no chance after death. There was no value in prayers for the dead, nor any purgatory where one could atone for sins done during life upon earth.

All this brought deeper preoccupations with his spiritual condition before God. Frank had always been looking for peace with God and forgiveness of sin. His spirit grew heavier within himself. The weight of his sin was causing deep concern to his soul.

Harry also told Frank about the "Rapture", the coming of the Lord to take His church to Himself, into heaven. All the believers who had trusted Christ as their Saviour could look forward to this event. There would be the sound of a trumpet from God and the Lord would come to the clouds. Believers who had died would experience resurrection and the ones still living upon the earth would have their bodies transformed into ones that were incorruptible. This story made a profound impression on Frank and he kept watching for this event, which no doubt brought him a sense of fear but as yet he wasn't ready to accept Harry's teachings.

Some time later, Frank was asleep one night in his bed when he was suddenly awakened by the tremendous roar of a trumpet which left him wondering if it was the "trump of God" of which he had read in the New Testament, and of which Harry had told him. He felt deeply disturbed by the thought, wondering if that was the end of the day of grace for sinners like himself.

In the morning, he rushed to work in the factory and looked around for Harry who wasn't at his usual place of work. The disturbing feeling inside him became more pronounced. "Has it happened? Is it possible that the sound I heard during the night was the trump of God? ... Have the Christians been "raptured", taken to heaven?"

These and many other questions kept whirling in his head that morning ... However, great was his relief when he saw Harry come back to his duties in the factory. Frank ran to him demanding to be told why he was so late! It turned out to be the simple matter of Harry taking the morning off for a doctor's appointment. But the experience made a serious impact on the young gang leader causing him to review his own position before God. Later on, he learned that the trumpet he had heard was an alarm warning of an air raid over Glasgow that took place that night! Without a shadow of doubt the experience left its mark on his spirit.

Harry continued to show Frank friendship, always speaking kindly to him and sharing a tasty bit out of his lunch box.

Then one Friday afternoon as Frank was standing by the machine well, still discussing and resisting, Harry said: "Frank, the important thing you have to realize is that God loves you and sent His Son for you!"

Frank said, "For me?"

Harry continued, "The Lord Jesus allowed Himself to be beaten, crowned with a crown of thorns for you."

"For me? Are you sure, Harry?" "Yes, Frank, the Lord Jesus was crucified for you", Harry answered.

"For me? He did it because He loves me?"

"Yes, Frank. The Lord loves you with an intense love."

Frank couldn't resist any longer and with tears in his eyes, standing by the machine well, he gave thanks to God for His great love for sinners like him and there and then accepted Christ as his personal Saviour.

Nothing had ever made such an impact on his heart as the truth of the love of God shown in Jesus Christ dying on the Cross out of love for a young gangster like him.

The rest of that afternoon in the factory Frank was walking in the clouds with the sheer happiness of having found peace with God, having his sins forgiven ... and being ready for the trump of God whenever it sounded.

After work, he made his way home and was crossing the street near his house when a large intercity bus whizzed by him, nearly hitting him. He was shaken by the experience. But he was more amazed at his reaction! In the past, his vile mouth would have shot out curses and swear words against the driver, but now he praised the Lord for the security of his salvation. The thought that came into his head was, "Another coat of paint and I would have been ushered into the presence of God. It would have been bliss! Forever with the Lord!" This confirmed to his heart that all the retreats of the past with their resolutions to do better could not change the heart of man. When Jesus comes into a person's heart, the Holy Spirit makes the change from inside.

## Chapter 4

# A NEW WAY OF LIFE

At the weekend, Frank went back to Mass as had been his custom for years. He found it empty. The ritual that was familiar to him from the past didn't touch his heart. Very disappointed with the service he went home wondering what was wrong with him.

The following weekend, as work finished in the factory, Frank walked together with Harry and asked him about his plans for the weekend. "What do you do with yourself on Sundays, Harry?"

Harry tactfully replied, "I get together with young people with common interests. Would you like to come with me? Afterwards we can both go to my home and have tea."

Frank said, "Are you sure? Will your wife have some of that delicious pie you bring at times?" "Yes", said Harry, "and what is more, you can have a whole pie for yourself!"

After this conversation, they made arrangements to meet in time to go with the young people Harry met with every Sunday afternoon (a Bible Study group). Frank went home wondering if those young people met to exchange stamps or perhaps other tricks just as he used to occupy himself during his Sundays.

Sunday afternoon he met with Harry and they went into a plain building called Summerfield Hall. Frank was well attired with his gang apparel. When he realized that this group of young people were of a different kind, he didn't take off his overcoat all afternoon. He was afraid of being rejected as he was wearing his gang clothes.

Afterwards, as Harry had promised, they made their way to his home, where they had tea, Frank enjoying every moment of it. Gena had set a nice table and presented good home baking; a treat for young Frank. Interesting to note that the gang habits he had absorbed caused young Frank to look at their house noticing how easy it would be to break in and what things would be worth stealing. He rejected the thought as his heart had been changed at conversion. It takes some time to re-programme the thought life!

The time to part came and Harry said his goodbye to Frank, but Frank quickly interjected and said, "I heard there was another gathering in the evening. Can I not come?" This was sweet music to Harry who was overjoyed to perceive the Holy Spirit working in Frank. Frank went along with him to the evening gathering at Summerfield Hall. Everybody was very polite to the visitor, and he was urged to take off his overcoat since the hall was nice and warm. Frank finally took his coat off and sat down. People were taken aback to see this young gang member from the tenements of Glasgow sitting in their midst. But, wisely, they showed welcoming love to the stranger who had come in to listen to the Bible teaching.

That night the speaker was Mr. Petrie and he was giving a series of teaching sessions on the Tabernacle. (The portable sanctuary made by Moses as instructed by God.) The theme that first night was, "Look that thou make them after their pattern, which was shewed thee in the mount" (Exodus 25:40). Frank sat there and listened enthralled as the speaker developed the truths concerning the building of the Tabernacle. For some obscure reason he was able to enter fully into the teaching and it was heavenly food for his newly "born again" soul. He had an unusual gift to understand obscure portions of the Bible and explain them.

As the meeting came to a close, again he sought Harry and asked if he would be allowed to return the next night until the preacher finished his series of teaching services. So Frank was there every night. He hated "wasting" time in singing and praying. His thirst for Scripture teaching was tremendous. At the end of the week of meetings, he knew he had found "the Way, the Truth and the Life". He went home and dropped the bombshell on his father's lap. "Dad, I am not going back to the Catholic Church. I have found the place where my soul will be nurtured and refreshed."

Mr. Haggerty looked horrified at his son's statement. He had become a turncoat, a traitor, a disgrace to his faith. Quickly he ordered him out of the house. He was not to return home until he repented of this silly idea and decided to return to the Roman Catholic Church.

Frank went out, rejoicing because he was suffering for his faith and for his Saviour Jesus Christ. After all, the Lord had suffered crucifixion to save him from his sin and guilt. He found refuge in an abandoned school and that was where he spent some nights. In the meantime, his father was frantically looking for his son until he found him and asked him to return home. Mr. Haggerty noticed the changes that were taking place in his son and had to accept that this "conversion" was doing wonders for his behaviour, not least on his florid vocabulary!

Mr. Haggerty deeply resented the influence of the "Bible people" in his son's life. Once when Harry Burness went to visit Frank, Mr. Haggerty started complaining to him about certain things he disliked in his son. Frank heatedly started defending the Christians in Summerfield Hall, and specially his spiritual father. But Harry was a wise person and proceeded to advise Frank about showing more respect toward his father. This disconcerted Frank for a moment, and had a beneficial effect on Mr. Haggerty, as he realized that the "Bible people" weren't out to rob him of his son but they were out to make him a better man. It also helped to lessen the antagonism against the "Bible people", and he accepted the invitation to visit Summerfield Hall and did so occasionally.

Frank became a frequent guest at Harry's home. He enjoyed discussing Bible themes with his mentor, who instructed him in the Scriptures, and was able to instil in Frank a love for deep Bible study and good Christian literature, a love which lasted throughout Frank's life.

There was a young fellow in Summerfield Hall about the same age and build as Frank. Jack was the only son of Mr. and Mrs. Budge. Both became close friends and the Budges virtually adopted Frank as another son seeing that both young fellows had become inseparable.

Mr. Budge was a man of prayer. He had been a train engineer, but eventually became a tramcar driver for the City of Glasgow

Corporation because it gave him odd hours of shift work which allowed him to dedicate time to prayer. Throughout many years Mr. Budge prayed three times a day on behalf of Frank, first as a young convert, then for his exercise to go abroad as a missionary, and continued praying faithfully when Frank became a missionary in Bolivia. This went on until the time when he went to be with the Lord.

*(On one occasion when Frank went back on furlough to Scotland, he mentioned the need of effective prayer on behalf of missionaries and gave the example of Mr. Budge who until that time had prayed faithfully for Frank and his family. He calculated that he had done so over 45,000 times, and that this had been a source of strength for himself and the family along the years.)*

As time passed, Frank discovered the doctrine of Believer's Baptism and so was baptized in Summerfield Hall and added to the fellowship. He also became fearlessly involved in all the activities in the assembly and completely gave up his gang connections since their activities were going the opposite direction to a Christian life.

When the call for Military Service came in 1943, he realized he could not enlist in any services that would demand harming or taking the lives of men and women. He pled to be excused as a Conscientious Objector on account of his faith. He accepted willingly the imposed penalty of building temporary military shelters in a labour camp, praising the Lord for the freedom to appeal for a decision that would not harm human lives by his hand.

Frank developed spiritually in the fellowship at Summerfield

Hall. During that time he realized he had to share with others the good news of salvation and peace with God. He managed to get a group of young tough fellows from the neighbourhood to attend. Their delight had been in coming in to disturb the Children's meetings at the hall. He nicknamed them the "Tough Monkeys." The youngsters were so proud of their new status that they stopped making themselves a nuisance to the others! Frank used the same method that Harry Burness had used, inviting them to his house for a meal from time to time to create a friendship with them. Frank would cook easy meals for them.

*(Years later his wife challenged him about his cooking at that time. Frank always maintained he didn't cook at home because he even burned the water! In truth, he had prepared himself for missionary life in such a way that food was accepted with pleasure, but he was not a slave to food, meaning he would go without if need be ... Luckily, his wife enjoyed cooking and baking! Also, he was ready to accept the worst meal with thanksgiving. A very important trait for missionaries who touch all layers of society.)*

Another special activity at Summerfield Hall was the choir and Bible Study group for young people. Once a week they would get together to go to Dr. Manderson's in Bearsden for the Bible Study night.

One Monday night the group were going to Dr. Manderson's in Bearsden and when they got to Anniesland Cross it started raining heavily. They felt discouraged by the weather and so quickly made the decision to get shelter from the rain by going into the nearby gospel hall, Anniesland Hall, where a well-known speaker was having special meetings for young people. As Mr. Dennis Barnes developed his message, Frank's heart was touched and he started thinking about his parents and their lost condition before God. Ever since he trusted the Lord in the factory he had been very burdened about his Dad, who though he was a good church man, yet he still had his faith in the rituals of the church and not in the Saviour Jesus Christ.

As he listened, his mind switched to his mother. She had died when Frank was only five years old. As far as he knew, she had never heard the news of salvation through faith in Christ. Frank started wondering about her spiritual state and realized it was too late to reach her. The thought had never crossed his mind when he was following the Roman Catholic faith. But as he listened to Dennis, the reality of being too late filled his heart with sadness and he started mourning afresh for his mother, but with a different pain, the pain of knowing nothing more could be done to help her soul. As the meeting came to a close, the young people filed out, but Frank was overtaken with the pain of grieving for his mother and was slow to leave. Dennis Barnes noticed the troubled look in the young man and told him to wait behind for a little chat. As Dennis questioned him, Frank expressed his deep sadness about his mother's lost condition and his pain about her being beyond reach.

Dennis wisely directed his thoughts to the present and challenged him to give his life to the Lord's service in order to reach people who could still be reached. He told Frank to start preparing himself by learning Bible doctrines as much as possible. Also by making himself available for any kind of spiritual work that needed to be done. He impressed on Frank the need to be exercised in prayer, seeking God's will for his life.

The experience of that night changed Frank from a fun-loving young man to a serious person who realized the importance of reaching out to the lost before it is too late for salvation. It left a mark in him for the rest of his life.

That same night Frank realized that God had brought a new direction into his life. He was willing to place his life on the altar for the Lord to use him as a missionary abroad or to stay at home, but was committed to living a fully consecrated life in service for God from that time onwards.

*(A week after he had arrived in Bolivia, Frank accompanied Mr. Horne, who was in the country as a missionary, to a funeral. A man who had been quite friendly with the missionaries had passed away, the wife and daughters were desolate and loudly lamenting the loss of the beloved husband and father. Friends of the family were very concerned about the wife and were afraid she would suffer a collapse at the time when the coffin would be taken out of the house to go to the cemetery. It was agreed that someone would distract the grieving widow at that point. Unfortunately, she and her daughters heard the noise of the car starting, and she forced her way among the crowd, throwing herself on the coffin and crying, "Lo hemos perdido! Lo hemos perdido!"*

*Frank asked Mr. Horne: "What is she saying?" When Mr. Horne translated the words, "He is lost to us", Frank's thoughts went back to that night in Anniesland Hall when he realized that his mother was forever lost to him, and how he had been struck by the importance of reaching people while they can be saved. Once people pass the boundary of death, they are forever lost to us. We have no tomorrows nor yesterdays, only today. "Seek ye the Lord while He may be found.")*

*Chapter 5*

# GUIDANCE AND PREPARATION

From that time on, Frank gave much time to preparing himself for service. He was encouraged by the elders in the assembly to study the Bible in preparation for future service. At the same time, they brought good Bible teachers to the assembly who provided excellent Bible teaching and gave a good foundation in the Scriptures. This enabled him to become a good teacher and preacher himself in his work as a missionary in Bolivia and elsewhere.

The next step was to look for definition and guidance as to a future sphere of service. Reading books available to him his interest was at first directed to China, then India, but he had no definite leading. Then someone gave him a book, "Adventures with the Bible in Brazil". The title "Adventures" was a definite lure for the ex-gang leader. Around that time, Frank was confined to bed with double pneumonia and forbidden to even put a hand out from under the bed covers, since his condition was quite serious. Mr. Haggerty propped the open book on the bed for Frank to read, but of course he wasn't around to turn the pages and

Frank read the same page over and over till he almost memorized the book with the result that Frank's search was redirected and focused on South America. But where in South America? It is a large continent with about a dozen different countries. Again there was a period of seeking the Lord's will.

The assembly at Summerfield Hall was very interested in missionary work. Missionaries would come and give a report about their work so the young people were regularly presented with a challenge to serve abroad.

Around the latter part of 1947, a missionary, Mr. Peter Horne, visited Summerfield Hall to give a report of the progress of the Gospel work in the land of Bolivia where he and his wife had been labouring for many years. Mr. Horne was a very sick man and before he finished his report had to sit down. Frank, who was in the gathering, was filled with compassion for the dear missionary and felt someone should go and help relieve his burden on the field. That same night someone asked Mr. Horne if he was going to retire from the field on account of his health. Mr. Horne answered with a tired but firm voice, "No! ... We are returning to the work in Bolivia. There are many perishing souls who still need the Gospel of salvation."

Frank was impressed by the man, his devotion to the Lord and dedication to the very difficult work. There was much opposition to Evangelicals in those years. Bolivia had been in the grip of Roman Catholicism since the Spanish conquistadores arrived in South America.

As Frank was going out, he shook hands with Mr. Horne who, looking right into his eyes, said clearly, "Young man, I give you an invitation to come to Bolivia!" After that short exchange, Frank went home feeling he had been given food for thought. Hadn't he been trying to find direction as to which country in South America he should serve God in? Was this a message from the Lord? Was Bolivia the country that God had chosen for his sphere of service? Later in the night, he realized he didn't know where that man was living. He should have asked for his address. Perhaps he could get more information!

During the following months, Frank found himself  unable to find any details about Mr. Horne.  No one seemed to know where the Hornes were living during their period of furlough in Scotland. They seemed to have disappeared from the map. (This was probably because he was unable to take report meetings due to his poor health.)

The following summer, the young people of Summerfield Hall formed a Tract Band and went giving out tracts seeking to evangelize people in the villages and towns around Glasgow.

One particular weekend they went to Strathaven, a village in Lanarkshire.  After giving out gospel tracts around the village, they continued walking toward the farms, visiting every house on the road. They arrived at a dairy farm called "Hall of Kype Farm", and  across from the farm there was an attractive cottage. The group divided, some went to the farm and Frank went to the cottage.  After knocking at the door, a woman opened the door, took a look at Frank, and before he had a chance to say a word, she yelled in a loud voice, "Peter ... Peter!" She then ran inside banging the door right on Frank's nose, leaving him completely surprised since he didn't know the woman.  He couldn't understand why she had reacted so violently when she had seen him.

He was wondering what to do next, whether he should knock again or join his friends who were across the road at the farm. Suddenly the door opened and to Frank's amazement the elusive Mr. Horne was smiling and extending a hand of welcome!

Mrs. Horne, who had opened the door at first, said, "Peter, this is the young man you mentioned meeting at Summerfield Hall?" ... "Isn't he?" "Welcome ... Welcome! ... Come in ... We would like to have a chance to speak to you!"

After so many months of fruitless inquiries about the whereabouts of the missionary couple, he had found them most unexpectedly. After the introduction, the group were invited in for tea and had a very nice and informative visit, which for Frank was exactly what he had been looking for in his search for guidance as to where the Lord would have him go.

*Frank Haggerty preaching*

Poor Frank, in his eagerness he thought he would be away to Bolivia within the next few months.

He said to Mr. Horne, "What will I do if I get there before you do?" Mr. Horne simply smiled.

The young Glasgwegian had much to learn before he was ready to leave the home shores to face the difficulties in the mission field. This quite apart from getting grounded in the Scriptures which would be the biggest demand in years to come.

Following this almost miraculous encounter, Frank realized he had received very clear leading from God concerning the place He would have him serve as a missionary. He communicated this exercise to the elders at Summerfield Hall, expecting to be sent to the field immediately. Great was his surprise when Mr. Thompson asked quite bluntly: "Frank, what language do they speak in Bolivia?"

Frank said, "Spanish, Mr Thompson!" To which he said, "Frank, you can't speak English properly. How can you expect to learn Spanish?"

It was like a bucket of ice water dumped on his head! However, Mr. Thompson continued: "I advise you to go and take a good course in English before you tackle your learning of Spanish!"

Frank realized that in spite of his bluntness, Mr. Thompson wanted the best preparation for him in his new role as a "missionary-on-training". Another thing he tried to impress on Frank was the fact that the missionary goes to the new country to preach the Gospel, leading people to salvation by faith, not to change Bolivians into Scottish men like himself. Frank got this message! In later years he respected the ethnicity of the Bolivian people to the utmost!

The dear men at Summerfield Hall knew that his broad Glasgow accent and slangy speech would not be acceptable to present the Gospel, nor would it help in learning the nuances of another language. He understood that English grammar was a requirement to help him with language learning, and he also needed Spanish lessons. They were very glad to see this development in the young man, especially considering his background.

(*Harry Burness, an important mentor to him, eventually moved with his family to the North of Scotland and he went into full-time service as an Evangelist visiting the small towns in that part of Scotland. His ministry was greatly appreciated.*)

For the next four years, the elders concentrated on preparing Frank, guiding him to learn different skills. At the same time he was able to complete his studies at Stowe College on building and carpentry which would be a big asset in his missionary service. Frank not only was used to build the Church of Christ spiritually, but also had an exercise to build meeting halls where the Gospel message could be faithfully preached.

One of the important lessons he learned was about stewardship of money. On one occasion he went to listen to a preacher who spoke about money, showing that giving is a gift everybody has. Every person has some money in his pocket, and can use it for themself or for God. Money can be the thing that will enslave a person unless it is surrendered to God.

Frank placed his penny fare in the offering and walked home profoundly touched by the teaching which changed his attitude to money to the end of his life. Until that time he had been working hard, trying to earn good money. He was quite ambitious to get on in life, hoping to acquire a position in society. His prayer from that time on was that God would take that ambition from his heart and replace it with a giving spirit.

In relation to this experience, he was known as a good worker, well appreciated by his employer. Shortly before the way cleared for Frank to go abroad, his boss unexpectedly called and spoke to him offering him a partnership in the firm. What a temptation! But God had already cleansed out the original ambition and Frank could gladly say that it was more important to serve God than to serve for money.

From the time he made known his calling to be a missionary to the elders in Summerfield Hall, Frank entered into all the activities of the assembly and other evangelistic outreaches. He delighted going to Open Air meetings, specially going to the back courts of the tenement houses around the Hall, Tract Bands, Gospel Campaigns ... anywhere in and around Glasgow.

Mr. Wilding had been a missionary in Africa. He also went to Brazil and finally he was working in evangelistic outreach in Scotland. He was a very active man with campaigns in different towns and villages. A group of enthusiastic young people joined and accompanied him in these outreaches.

Frank also joined the group that accompanied Mr. Wilding to reach out in villages in Lanarkshire. There was a mining community in the Douglas area. Miners everywhere are hard workers, hard living, hard drinkers. Often Christianity is a sissy word for them.

The reputation that surrounded Douglas village challenged Mr. Wilding to go to the area, taking the message of the Gospel. Among the group of young helpers, Frank found himself invited. He was attracted by Mr. Wilding's personality. He was a tenderhearted man, caring, and deeply concerned about people's spiritual well being. Always smiling, soft spoken and friendly.

The helpers had to bring a small tent, just the necessary wherewithal, and be prepared to sleep under the stars, and look after themselves. They were to join in all the activities during the campaign. In other words, tough work for everyone. They were stationed in the village of Greengairs, helping in the small assembly there at the same time as they did door to door evangelism.

In the mining area they visited all the homes with tracts and toward the end of the day they held Open Air meetings, just as people were coming out from work in the mine. As usual, there were plenty of hecklers. There was one evening when one of the miners was particularly nasty and offensive, specially against the Lord's person. Mr. Wilding suddenly stopped and addressed himself to the man with the following: "Man, be careful how you speak. You don't know what tomorrow will bring." Very soon after that, the meeting was closed and everybody went their own way.

The following day, the group made their way back to Douglas village again. As they entered the village, they perceived a change in the atmosphere. Then, they saw people hanging around the place where they usually had the Open Air meeting. Several approached Mr. Wilding sad but angrily asking: "How did you know? Why did you say that?" Many other questions were thrown at him. He was confused at the situation.

Later on, the full story came out. Apparently the heckler returning to work that morning was short tempered and didn't wait for the other workers to descend into the depths of the mine. He activated the cage (lift) to go by himself. Half way down something gave way and the cage went out of control and crashed down to the bottom. The man was dead when the rescuers managed to go down! Naturally everybody was wondering why Mr. Wilding had spoken that way!

This had an effect on several people in the village. Attitudes against the Gospel changed and several people trusted the Lord as Saviour. The team were happy to know that several persons were saved and on their way to heaven. They felt rewarded for answered prayer.

In Greengairs the group were able to see good results in the asssembly. Many were added where they continued faithfully. Frank had a special link with the Bell and Rae families who maintained prayerful contact with him over the years.

Franks's interest in another aspect of Christian work was stimulated in the following way. One night he was walking home and met a friend on Dumbarton Road, Glasgow. Both continued walking together and exchanging news. Jimmy Duffus said he was worried because his brother was running a Camp for young fellows and one of the key counsellors couldn't make it to the Camp because of some illness. He asked Frank if he was free to help. Frank accepted the invitation and joined the group. There was another young Christian called Jim McNeill who would be helping as well. The young campers were a rowdy group but met their match in the ex-gang leader who knew how to handle toughs. They all had a very challenging week, and toward the end of the camp six young fellows had trusted the Lord as Saviour. There was much rejoicing over the results. At that camp Frank teamed up with Jim McNeill, who became a life-long prayer partner.

Work like this was not without its humourous side. As Frank and Jim were clearing the camp they found a packet of rice and a good amount of milk left over. They decided to make rice pudding. Neither knew how to cook rice. They emptied the packet into the pot and added milk. "Frank, bring another pot." "Jim, bring more milk, another pot ... more milk!" They ended up with pots and pots of rice pudding. They always chuckled at the words "rice pudding". Jim would say: "Frank, remember the rice pudding?" and both would explode with laughter!

A love for camp work was born at that time. However, the sobering lesson came later because some of those young men were dead within six months, and sad to say among them was one who rejected Christ. Once again there was impressed on Frank's heart the urgency of reaching people before it is too late.

Another blessing that came into his life was the fact that his father eventually realized that he also needed to have a personal relationship with God, trusted the Lord Jesus as his Saviour, and joined the fellowship at Summerfield Hall. The friendly attitude of the believers and the loving friendship demonstrated by them helped to ease the absence of his son when he left for Bolivia.

Likewise Frank had peace to go knowing that Mr. Haggerty was in the Lord's hands, no matter what would take place during the period of absence from one another. As a matter of fact, Frank never saw his father again, as his Dad passed away before Frank returned to Scotland on his first furlough.

## Chapter 6

# SAILING TO THE NEW WORLD

Frank at times grew impatient with the lengthy 4-year preparation to become a missionary. Then, at last, he was summoned to meet with the elders who, now satisfied with his progress, commended him to the Lord's service in Bolivia and elsewhere. It was a wonderful day for Frank to receive this commendation from the assembly. It would open doors and give the assurance of fellowship and prayer that would go with him to his new sphere of service for God.

The next step was to secure a berth in a boat bound for South America, so he went to speak to Mr. McFarland, a Christian travel agent, who mentioned the "Reina del Pacífico", a passenger boat that went to Arica in Chile. Mr. McFarland kindly booked a ticket for Frank who could only put down a deposit since he had used most of his money to buy equipment he would need. Those days were days of faith, learning to look to the Lord for His provision toward the payment that had to be paid by a certain date. Money was very scarce and hard to come by because by this time he had already left his secular job.

Still no money to pay for the boat ticket. The deadline was drawing near. "Lord ... is this the time to go?" "Do I have to wait for the next boat?" "Lord, have I moved out of Your will?" Such were his anxious prayers. Worrying days for both Frank and Mr. McFarland, since he had put himself out by keeping the ticket open.

In Summerfield Hall a box had been placed with Frank's name to receive gifts of fellowship from the Christians in the congregation. Finally, the day came when the box was opened and Frank was given the money collected. Amazingly, it came to exactly the amount of money owed to the travel agent. Frank quickly went to pay Mr. McFarland and picked up his tickets for the boat. In this wonderful way God confirmed to Frank that in spite of the difficulties and anxieties that come in the course of life, He is over all and will give adequate provision for the need.

With the fare paid, the departure date was announced and invitations were sent out for friends to gather in Summerfield Hall to bid farewell to Frank.

He was very encouraged to see a large number of friends from different assemblies in and around Glasgow gathered for that meeting to pray and commend the young missionary to the Lord in his new venture and to bid him Godspeed. The memory of these loving friends commending him to the Lord remained in Frank's memory to encourage him throughout the many difficult days of adapting to life in the new country.

Ian Campbell, a close friend, came and when he shook hands he placed a £10.00 note in his hand. Later Frank learned that this gesture was called a "missionary handshake." He felt it would be exactly what he needed to pay for his train ticket from Glasgow to Liverpool the next day to catch the boat "Reina del Pacífico."

When Frank arrived at Central Station in Glasgow, he met Ian Horne, Mr. Peter Horne's son, who had come to give Frank a parcel for his parents. Out of the blue Ian decided to accompany Frank in the train and he bought tickets for both of them with sleeping berths so they could have a restful night. They had a good time together and it was a really nice send-off.

The £10.00 note was still in Frank's pocket, and he wondered what was coming next. But very soon he found out. The Port Authorities demanded payment for storing Frank's baggage for a couple of days - the cost was exactly £10.00! God had already provided for the need. Now everything was ready for departure and he found the cabin that would be his abode for the next 5 weeks.

At that time there was an embargo on money going out of Britain. A person was allowed to take only £5.00 out of the country. Frank had his £5.00 which needed to be stretched out to last him for the duration of the trip to South America and on to his destination in Santa Cruz, Bolivia.

Frank sailed from Liverpool on January 7th 1951 on the trip that would take him to Bolivia to continue his service for the Lord. As the ship left British shores, he was meditating on God's goodness to him since the day he trusted the Lord Jesus as his personal Saviour. As the "Reina del Pacifico" slowly left the harbour, he stood on deck looking at his homeland receding into the distance and praising God for the wonderful change He had wrought in his life. He was beginning the trip to the greatest adventure of his life!

Frank couldn't help remembering his school friend, John Grey, who had ended his life in the prison at 24 years old, the same age as Frank. He had been a friend of Frank's for a long time. Both went to the same school, and for a period shared the same desk. Later they were often together during Frank's days of youthful "gangsterism".

Unfortunately John Grey had continued in a life of crime. One night he and a companion broke into a workshop to steal some goods. When the watchman found them, John Grey struck him very hard, resulting in his death later in hospital. John Grey and his friend were caught and taken to prison. The case made big news in the city and people were clamouring for justice for the poor watchman.

Ultimately, John Grey was sentenced to death by hanging and in September 1950 he went to the gallows. He would be buried in a special lot in the prison yard reserved for criminals condemned to death. There would be no plaque to mark his burial. The only reminder of his life would be his initials "J.G." written on the wall in Barlinnie prison.

John Grey, who served the prince of this world and his own self, finished in an unknown grave. Frank, a young gang leader saved from a life of crime, was now sailing to serve the King of kings. Frank Haggerty had been on the same path as John Grey, yet, after he found Jesus Christ as Saviour, his life had been completely changed from a life of crime against society and fellow humans to a life serving God and seeking to help people. Only God can change lives and transform men and women to make them useful to others around them.

Aboard the ship Frank met a Polish engineer who was travelling to take a job in Bolivia. Mickey became a close friend to Frank. Every evening he treated the young missionary to a glass of Coke and both sat chatting over it. Mickey was an avowed Roman Catholic but would listen to Frank's stories and his testimony of his relationship with God.

There was also a Salvation Army missionary couple, the McK's, in the same boat travelling to Chile. As believers, they gravitated to one another and formed a Christian friendship during the long trip. When the boat arrived in Bermuda, people who had money could go out for the day, but it meant having to use a small launch to go ashore. Frank looked at the attractive shore but wisely decided to keep holding on to his pennies. He was quite surprised when Mr. McK. came to invite him to go ashore with them. They had received 7 tickets to get the family to go ashore to join a Salvation Army march in honour of the missionaries. Frank accepted the invitation and took little Terry McK. on his shoulders. Great was his surprise when he discovered the dear Salvation Army Bermudans would not consider him walking at the side of the march, so he was included in the whole procession!

He felt uncomfortable being in the middle of the celebrations, but gratefully accepted this provision of fellowship in the Lord. The Christian folks in Bermuda were very friendly and plied the missionaries with enough tropical fruit to last them for the rest of the trip.

After thirty two days sailing, the ship arrived at Arica, Chile. The group had to part company with Frank continuing to his destination in Bolivia. Before he left on the train, the Salvation Army couple asked him to deliver some musical instruments to other missionaries in Bolivia and gave him money to pay for transporting them. They didn't realize that this money was the amount needed to pay for the train ticket to La Paz and the airplane ticket to Santa Cruz! Two days after his arrival he had his 25th birthday. He was ready to start the life of a missionary.

Once again these experiences strengthened Frank's conviction and his dependence on the Lord to lead him along the new life of service in Bolivia. Frank never asked for any money for himself and his activities in the Lord's work. He would present the needs of other needy people or situations, but never for himself or his family.

*(Many years later, he was teaching how God will provide the necessary wherewithal to take His servants to their destination. He read from Philipians 1 and mentioned the events told above. It thrilled his heart to be able to testify of many wonderful small and large provisions that God had given day by day from the time he left his home in Glasgow until he arrived in Bolivia and then continued throughout his life of service as a missionary.)*

*Chapter 7*

# BOLIVIA: A NEW COUNTRY

In 1951, Bolivia was going through a very troubled time in its history. In the wake of the Great Depression, the humiliation of losing the 3-year Chaco War with Paraguay over a disputed border (1932-1935) and World War II, Bolivia was economically depressed with little capacity to participate in industry and trade. There was a flagrantly unequal distribution of power and resources, where a small elite (mostly of European descent) governed the country and owned large tracts of land, while the majority (mostly Indigenous people) were landless or subsistence farmers who were excluded from economic and political power.

Bolivian thinkers and politicians reflected the polarization between fascism and communism that emerged worldwide in the 1930s and 1940s, informing very different ways to address the economic and social woes of the country. In 1949, a strike by tin miners over their working conditions was put down by a brutal massacre ordered by the government aligned with the Tin Magnate, Patiño. This give rise to a brief civil war in Bolivia that pitted the uprising of the mostly indigenous workers (allied with communist tendencies) against the conservative mostly European-white elite. In May 1951 - just months after Frank arrived - the communist-leaning party was elected democratically, only to be overthrown by a military junta 10 days later, which in turn, was deposed in a coup d'état by the communist-leaning party one year later. The 1952 Revolution (as it is called) was a movement to bring the Indigenous people out of their downtrodden situation, but it was bloody revolution where many people died, many were put in prison and others had to abandon the country to preserve their lives. The people who came into power were determined to bring change to the country and in that determination they were ruthless during their 12 years of governance. This period brought much fear of persecution along with positive changes.

During the decade of the 1950s, the Government brought out several important reforms that began to change the face of the country, and brought the Indigenous population from obscurity and serfdom to a better life. A movement toward industry was also started. There were three important reforms that were implemented with profound consequences for Bolivia and for missionary work: 1) educational reform; 2) employment rights, and 3) agricultural reform.

First, educational reform made basic (primary) education a right for all and brought education to all corners of the land. In 1952, 60% of the population was illiterate, and 20% had only primary education. Schools were only available in urban areas. The educational reform established rural primary schools even in the remotest areas in order to give the children the basic skills of reading, writing and arithmetic to make them participants in the modern project, bringing them out of the stone age in which the adults had been living all their lives. If rural children wanted further education they needed to go to the cities and could continue studying to achieve a professional qualification providing they could meet the costs.

The education reform provided an opportunity for mission work. Rural schools were established with few resources. The New Testament was used as a reader in many country schools, so many missionaries - including Frank - took advantage of this situation and visited country schools with Bibles and New Testaments to give to teachers and children. The availability of the bilingual New Testament in Quechua and Spanish in 1954 further opened the opportunity. As the children learned to read, they read the New Testament to their parents in both languages, thus becoming little Bible messengers and heralds of the Gospel. For the first time the Quechua people, the majority Indigenous group, heard the Word of God in their own language.

Second, a series of measures were enacted to protect the working classes. Until that time workers did not have any protection against employers who abused their authority, exemplified by the tin mines where workers extracted metals in appalling conditions. This gave rise to the 1949 civil war and resulted in the creation of the first Workers' Union which formed the seed of the 1952 Revolution. In general, the working class in any sphere of employment worked under poor conditions. Unions began to have more say on behalf of workers, enabling them to work in better conditions. Laws were enacted to protect employees, giving them the right to holidays and other benefits. Another critical measure that supported worker benefits was the granting of universal suffrage in 1952. For the first time Indigenous peoples, illiterate persons and women were given the right to vote, and granted the status of full citizens.

The third reform put into action was the agrarian reform that made land available to all who applied for agricultural land to work for themselves and their families. One of the legacies of the Spanish Conquest was a system of vast land estates owned by a small elite. In 1952, 70% of the agricultural land was owned by 5% of the population, with semi-feudal arrangements with Native or Indigenous people being kept as serfs ('peones'), working on the land with little or no rights and in a state of permanent indebtedness. They were routinely oppressed by the land owners. While some land owners were kind to their servants, others were plain despots. The Native people lived in abject poverty, and never saw money since all their supplies were obtained at the store provided by the land owners. In addition to these miserable social conditions, the agricultural methods were inefficient and the lack of industrialization meant that Bolivia was not able to meet its own needs for food production.

The agrarian reform broke up the land estates and granted free land to those who worked the land, on the condition that it had to be worked for agriculture. But the agrarian reform and the lifting of serfdom also brought out into the open the deep resentment that had been hidden for centuries in the hearts of the Indigenous people, mainly the Quechua and Aymara of the Andean plateau. The proposed reform rolled out slowly, falling short of its utopian promises, provoking some dreadful and bloody abuse. In some cases, Indigenous workers rose up and invaded their landlords' properties, ransacking everything, even killing their landlords if they were near. Not having any idea how to plan sowing, they squandered and ate everything in sight, not realizing they were wasting seed that should have been used for the following year. It took several hard and long years to achieve a kind of balance and for the Government to train and help people in the jump from being serfs to learning how to work their own land. The agrarian reform also uncovered a terrible enmity between the Indigenous and the white people on account of the historical abuse and the atrocities perpetrated as part of the agrarian reform.

So Frank arrived in Bolivia at a key turning point for the country. New rights were granted for the majority, and the old privilege of the few was breaking. The governing party instituted critical reforms that began to help the country emerge from the dark ages and into the 20th Century. But the country was ruled with an iron fist that made it dangerous to express any opinion that could be interpreted as opposing the governing party. Everyone lived in fear of the "Political Control", the organ that repressed ruthlessly any opposition. Those were dark years in Bolivia. One had to lie quietly and go about one's own business and hope to pass unnoticed.

# Chapter 8

# ADJUSTING TO THE NEW COUNTRY

It was a period of adjustment in every sense. Frank left Scotland in winter, and arrived in Santa Cruz in the middle of summer in the Southern Hemisphere. He arrived first in La Paz, the capital city of Bolivia, an interesting city founded in an immense crater-like hollow in the middle of the flat expanse of the Andean Plateau, at an altitude of 13,000 feet above sea level. After visiting Scottish missionaries in that city, Mr. and Mrs. Sam Lander, Frank continued his trip to Santa Cruz, a small city in the lowlands of Bolivia, in the savannah bordering the Amazon jungle to the east.

He arrived in February 1951 two days before his 25th birthday. It had taken five long years of preparation to join Peter and Mima Horne who had now returned to the field. Now, it was time for the all-important step of Language Study. The ability to communicate the Gospel to the people depends largely on the spoken language, therefore it is a priority for any missionary to give time to language study.

The Hornes showed Frank the initial steps needed to orientate him in the new culture. They also directed him to a good

Spanish teacher. During the following months, Frank dedicated much time to learning the intricacies of the Spanish tongue. It is said that it takes the best part of one to two years to become adapted to a new language and culture. While dedicating long hours to language study, there was also a fair amount of time spent accompanying Mr. and Mrs. Horne to visit believers and following up on any contacts acquired while giving out tracts to people in the street.

At that time Santa Cruz, though it had city status, was only a small town with sandy streets, poor water supply and only a few hours of deficient electric light, hence the need for lamps. For evening meetings at night there were kerosene lamps to be lit up and benches to be moved out to the patio for the evening meetings, since the lamps increased the already tropical heat in the meeting room.

After months of intense study of the Spanish language, Frank felt it was time to practise the language he had acquired by speaking to people in the country. He decided to extend his efforts to reach people in the land estates ("haciendas") to the north of Santa Cruz. For that purpose he rented a horse, packed saddle bags with New Testaments and Gospel literature and set off to continue the great adventure of reaching people with the Gospel of salvation by faith in the Lord Jesus Christ.

He discovered that those who lived in the haciendas were very friendly. Often, he also found the land owners to be glad of the visit of the "gringo". For years it had been the practice of land owners in the lowlands to offer hospitality to foreigners who often became part of the family group, receiving hospitality and sharing their "know how" to improve things in the development of the farmlands. So as Frank went around the large haciendas he was well received. As usual there were exceptions to the rule! Once as he walked his horse inside the gate of a particular hacienda he found himself facing a gun pointed to his head by the owner! The man proceeded to inform him that he was a devout Roman Catholic and would not allow a "Protestant" to come and teach heresies to his workers. Should he see Frank inside his land ever again he could consider himself a dead "gringo"!

Each trip was a new experience for the adventurous Glaswegian. On one occasion when he was on the trail he was joined by a group on horseback heading toward the same destination. After talking about wild beasts that come out of the jungle to attack the lone traveller, they offered to lead the way. They went to the front leaving Frank to flank the group. Frank was very happy to have their company along the trail and felt grateful for a great bunch of people helping to guide him. The others were armed with machetes and guns, while all the "gringo" had with him was a short blade knife, but he felt well protected by his new friends!

*Transport in Bolivia*

When he arrived at his destination, he praised his companions for being so kind in going ahead of him, ready to brave the dangers of the bush! His friend burst out laughing and explained to Frank that that was no "disinterested" bravery in their going first since it is a well-known fact that the tiger or puma always goes for the last one in the convoy! It goes to show that there is a lot to learn in a new culture beyond language learning.

Frank had a tremendous thirst for adventure. He always felt that God had called him to fulfil a marvellous mission. Telling of the saving grace of God through faith in the Lord Jesus Christ was the greatest experiences a person could have. Yet at the same time, travelling by horseback to the north of Santa Cruz was very challenging and exciting. He was seeing and enjoying the amazing provision of God in his own life. Not just reading about adventures while comfortably sitting by the fireside but being able to trace God's hand in his life day by day.

He knew God's provision in many simple ways. For example, he would suffer stomach upsets at home, but never while he was away from home eating all kinds of food when visiting country believers! Likewise, as a youth he was terrified of the dentist, and one of his great fears was being out in the jungle and getting a toothache. Before leaving Scotland he considered having his teeth pulled out and replaced by dentures to avoid his nightmare of suffering from toothache in the jungle. Someone very wisely advised him against it since his teeth were strong and in a fine condition! In all his years on the mission field, he continued to ask the Lord to keep him free from toothache when travelling. God honoured that prayer to the full. Although he remained terrified of the dentist and toothaches, he never experienced toothaches of any kind while he was on trips out of town.

## Chapter 9

# THE GLASWEGIAN COWBOY!

As Frank became more familiar with the language and customs, he travelled further and started meeting believers in different areas. They often lived in isolated places, and welcomed a visit from missionaries. They were always happy to receive teaching from the Bible and enjoy some Christian fellowship. In those years, the Roman Catholic priest had a big sway with the people, and working through the land owners they made life difficult for professing evangelical believers.

Some missionaries from New Tribes (an organization dedicated to unreached people groups) asked Frank to visit new believers in the Nueva Moka plantation. So Frank made his way to Nueva Moka and met the small group of professing Christians who made him very welcome. Naturally he had to stay overnight since it was quite a distance from the city of Santa Cruz. That night after gathering around the Word of God, they all went to bed. His hosts had given him their bed and would not hear otherwise. As Frank went to bed, he found his pillow covered with a sparkling white pillowcase and he wondered how they had a new pillowcase ready at hand for him. In the morning he discovered the new pillow slip was the man's best shirt. What a token of hospitality!

Another purpose for his horseback travels was his love of tropical hardwoods. When Frank was studying carpentry at Stow College in Glasgow he learned all about fine timbers, and that attracted him to visit the different sawmills in northern Santa Cruz with a double purpose of taking the message of the Gospel to the many workers in the sawmills and being able to observe the production of fine timber, from the felling of the trees to the finished product. He was fascinated by the abundance of good timbers in spite of the poor processing methods and preparation.

He heard of a large sawmill in a place called Mineros, which was in a different direction from the Nueva Moka area. He took off on his horse and was travelling along the trail, but at one point the pathway divided in two. The trail he followed soon ended in the jungle. It must have been a hunter's trail because it led nowhere.

He realized he was lost in the thick jungle and after going around for a while he couldn't find a way out. Finally, he decided to spend the night in a clearing in the jungle since it was getting near sundown. He tied up his jungle hammock (with an integrated mosquito net), tethered his horse, and crawled into his hammock to stay out of the clouds of mosquitoes. In the morning, he woke up surprised to see blood oozing out of a bite in his leg. Being so tall, the hammock didn't protect him completely and part of his leg was exposed to a thirsty bat that got its fill during the night!

Worse yet - his horse had gone. During the night, it worked itself loose and took off for home. He had intended to give the horse its head, hoping it would find a way back to his corral. But now with no horse Frank realized he was truly stranded in the jungle. He climbed up a tall tree to see if he could spot a landmark to direct him back to civilization only to find even taller trees that didn't permit any visibility!

He was in a dire predicament. He started walking around trying to find a trail to lead him out, and then he found himself returning to the same spot. He tried slashing the bushes, but the same happened again and again.

After several failures it became apparent to Frank that he was lost beyond his own ability to find a way out. As the day progressed he ran out of drinking water. Scouting around he found a hollow with dirty muddy water. It looked like the pigs' drinking and bathing pond! He carefully strained the water with his handkerchief, put some Halazone tablets in it and drank the water accompanied with much prayer.

The day was coming to an end and he had to get into his hammock for the second night, planning a different strategy for the next day and commending his way and plans to the Lord. In the morning, he bundled his hammock and picked up the horse saddle and his tracts and Scripture portions and set off, carefully trying to mark his progress in the jungle and making as much noise as possible to frighten wild beasts away.

Suddenly he came on to a trail and found himself looking into a gun that was being pointed at him by a wild-looking man on horseback. The man was very surprised to see the tall "gringo" emerging from the bushes. He thought he was going to encounter a wild beast and was getting ready to shoot it for meat!

The amazing point in the event is that Frank was on a little trail crossing the bigger trail which the person on horseback was following. One moment sooner or later and they would have missed meeting one another and probably Frank would have continued lost in the jungle. He was fond of saying, "I could have become a modern Tarzan!"

The man had an interesting story of his own. He told Frank that he had set off toward a sawmill in the morning, when suddenly he had found himself travelling along a trail seldom used. Instead of turning back he had decided to continue on it hoping to find some game to kill for sustenance. Instead he had found a lost man who needed to be rescued and brought back to civilization. He didn't know that it was God Himself who had caused him to take that trail. God is the God of perfect timing! Again, Frank's faith was strengthened by this new experience.

Frank asked the man to help him return to a place where he could make his way home. Frank noticed he was an educated speaker, and the man told him he was in hiding for political reasons. The party in Government were seeking to kill him so he couldn't show himself near a town. He offered to take Frank to a friend's place who would be able to lead him out of the jungle. Naturally Frank was glad of any help to get back to Santa Cruz.

Eventually, both got to a clearing where there was a hut, and there by a table there was another shirtless man, wielding a big knife, his body covered with blood. He looked terribly threatening with the knife in his hand. Frank thought: "Oops, I am out of the frying pan, into the fire; this man brought me here to murder me."

But he was utterly mistaken. The other man was only

butchering an animal. Mosquitos and flies were pestering him and so he kept swatting them off with his bloodied hands, ending up covered in blood himself! Both men treated him kindly, gave him some food, and the second man eventually took him to the outskirts of the nearest village.

Frank then went to the place where he used to corral his horse and found it grazing there. He went and claimed it and after proving his rights he got his horse back. With a thankful heart he made his way back to the home in Santa Cruz. Frank was very grateful to the Lord for His amazing and timely rescue. The Lord doesn't need a Tarzan. He needs men and women who travel to tell people of God's saving love.

## Chapter 10

# UNFAMILIAR HAZARDS!

Frank was introduced not only to new people and customs but also to the local wildlife. In the tropical jungle of Santa Cruz there are many snakes ranging from the inoffensive green grass snakes and water snakes, to extremely poisonous snakes such as rattlers, corals, and many others. Most people are afraid of snakes. To this Glaswegian even the ordinary green grass snake was enough to provoke a shudder of fear.

On another horseback visit, Frank stayed with Miguel and his family in their one-room hut. After they had a devotional time, they all went to sleep. By this time, Frank normally took a bed roll with him, and this he stretched out on the floor. In the early morning Frank's ears picked up a small sound and he woke up. He opened his eyes and, with a shock, he saw Miguel brandishing a huge machete, looking at Frank with wild eyes. Frank thought, "My friend Miguel has gone mad! I am a dead man! He is going to murder me!" Miguel lunged forward. His machete landed beside Frank - and on a deadly snake that was ready to bite the unsuspecting Frank. He had managed to kill a "Yoperohobobo" (Bothrops, a Bolivian lance-head pit viper), a poisonous snake that is attracted to human habitations seeking warmth. Miguel had seen the snake and had to act quickly to protect Frank from a deadly bite. Far from murdering him, Miguel saved Frank's life.

Another time, Frank was sleeping in Miguel's hut when he heard a little rattling noise which he was sure sounded like a rattler snake. Recalling the incident with Miguel and his machete, he thought: "Another snake!" He started calling in a whisper: "Miguel ... Miguel!" and stayed very still.

Finally Miguel woke up and said: "What is it, don Francisco?"

Frank said: "Miguel, there is a cascabel (rattler snake) near my head!" Miguel struck a match and lit up the "mechero," (a little kerosene wick lamp) and looked around for the rattler. Suddenly he burst out laughing. The noise was coming from the newly hatched chicks sheltering under the mother hen! Frank was quite relieved to hear this. Nevertheless, he remained very wary of snakes.

Sometimes missionary experiences range from the sublime to the ridiculous! But Frank's sensitivity to rattlers was on his mind through the experience of one of his new friends.

Frank met John Spiegel when he first arrived in Santa Cruz and knew him pretty well. John was a German who came to Bolivia in search of a different life style. He settled in Santa Cruz and would work wherever there was an opening in the country areas. Usually he was employed as a personnel manager in sawmills. The owners liked him because he managed to get good production from the workers.

He had a hammock strung up in a palm-roofed shack where he took his siesta after lunch. The siesta break is usually taken in the middle of the day to rest a little during the hottest period of the day in the tropical weather of the lowlands of Bolivia.

One afternoon after the midday meal, John was relaxing in his hammock when his eyes spotted a rattlesnake coming down toward him along the rope of the hammock. He was paralyzed by fear as there was no way he could shake the snake off without being bitten. John was well acquainted with the snakes in the bush and held them in fearful respect. The snake crawled over John's body and, sensing his heartbeat, felt "relaxed" and coiled itself on his stomach to enjoy a "snake siesta". John was unable to move.

The whistle for returning to work went, but John remained as still as possible. After a couple of hours, the workers were wondering what had happened to the "boss" since he was always very punctual. They said among themselves: "The Patron (Boss) is enjoying a long siesta!" Eventually one of them decided to go and check up to see if there was something wrong with the "patron". He walked into the shack and then he saw the look of terror in John's face as he mouthed: "Help! Help!"

The worker quickly went out and ran to tell the other workers what was happening with the "boss". One of the workers, who was a good shot, devised a plan. The first worker got his gun ready and a second worker started to tap gently on the hammock rope with a stick to awake the snake from its siesta. Disturbed, the snake raised up its head getting ready to strike. At that moment the other fellow fired his gun and blew the snake's head away. John was sweating profusely with the tension of having a sleepy snake resting on his stomach. Thanks to the good marksmanship of the man, he lived to tell the story.

Unfortunately, John was a skeptic and never showed any interest in Frank's message of the Gospel. Though, many years later his son became a Christian after being enslaved to drugs.

A useful snake is the "boyéh" (Boa) which is a carnivorous but non-poisonous snake that is quite favoured by farmers because they feed on rats and field mice that can be pests. Farmers try to attract them to live in places where corn and rice are stored to keep the place clear of rats which would otherwise waste the crop. They grow quite long and look fearsome to the onlooker.

I, Blanquita, remember a scene in childhood when the family was farming out in the country. I was about 10 years old and I was coming out of the banana grove. At the side of the path I spotted a large snake attracting a bird which was already mesmerized and couldn't move. In my innocence I called a "peon" and ordered him to kill the snake. Then very proudly dragging the dead snake which was probably five feet long I took it to the house to show father my achievement, expecting a word of praise. Great was my chagrin when father chided me for killing his prized snake which kept the fields free of unwanted vermin!

*Chapter 11*

# NED MEHARG, FELLOWSHIP IN THE WORK

In the same year Frank arrived in Bolivia, so did a young Australian missionary commended by assemblies in Australia. Ned Meharg arrived in June 1951. He joined Ron and Mavis Randall, missionaries who were labouring in Villazon, a border town on the southern limit of Bolivia with Argentina in the high Andean plateau or "Altiplano".

The Bolivian Altiplano is quite arid and desert-like. The climate is cold year-round due to the high altitude. The cold is relieved by the constant sunshine in daytime. There is no rainfall for most of the year. Rain comes during the summer months and often it turns to snow. The growing season is short and production sparse. Trees don't usually grow in the high altitude areas. There is only low brush or scrub. Consequently, trees are cared for and protected in places where they manage to survive.

*(I, Blanquita, remember a truck-driver friend who swerved into a tree in the Altiplano to avoid hitting a child who was on the road. The tree was demolished but the boy's life saved. But the city authorities fined Louis for the crime he had committed against the tree; it was a*

*higher fine than he would have had to pay to the family, had he hit the child!*)

Through the generations people born at high altitudes have developed chest and lung conditions that enable them to live in the thin air with less oxygen than people from lower altitudes. High altitude can be very harsh for all who live there, but specially people born at lower altitudes. The young Australian had difficulty adapting to the extreme cold of the Altiplano, a drastic change from the climate of his homeland.

Frank and Ned met at a Spanish language school in the city of Sucre, in the centre of Bolivia. Like Frank, Ned Meharg faced the arduous task of language learning, but language study was hard for Ned. As a young man he left school early to work and earn a living since his father was laid low with heart disease. He was a very practical handyman, a hard worker in every sense, but not a natural student. Yet since he felt the Lord would have him serve as a missionary, he had to get himself equipped for the mission field.

From the time Frank and Ned met, they felt they were like David and Jonathan whose souls were knit to one another (1 Samuel 18:1). Both men liked travelling and for them there was no better challenge than visiting areas untouched by the Gospel. As they became more fluent in the Spanish language, they started planning various activities in evangelistic outreach. Together they planned a trip to a region to the interior of Tupiza following the river San Juan de Oro, visiting the settlements along the river, giving out tracts and selling Scripture portions as well as speaking to everyone they met.

Ned's Australian expertise came in very handy in equipping them for the long trip. They got mules loaded with Scriptures and foodstuffs and set off from Tupiza, on a trip that took 26 days. As they neared the lower valleys, they reached the onion harvest time. People wanted to have Scripture portions but had no money, so the friends exchanged Scriptures for onions or an occasional egg. Their culinary ingenuity was tested to the utmost in finding ways to cook onions in appetizing ways!

Working with the mules was quite a job, especially for the Glaswegian born and brought up in city life who knew nothing about mules. His mule turned out to be a very stubborn animal so it got nicknamed Noggin. Poor Frank, he had a lot of difficulties with Noggin.

Once when they were fording the river, Noggin decided to sit in the water and would not move on. Frank had to hold its head up to stop his mule from committing suicide! After Ned got across the river, he quickly returned to help Frank unload the packs of Bibles and Scriptures. They had to stay there for a full day to dry out everything! Plastic wrap or bags were not available then!

Most people received the reading matter gladly. However, often the priest would come and make a bonfire of the literature of the "accursed Protestants". In one village, a little old woman wanted the Word of God so much she asked for a New Testament for her grandson to read it to her. She didn't have any money, but she brought two fresh brown eggs to pay for the "little book" which could tell her about God. When the priest came around gathering all the literature from the missionaries, she hid hers, denied getting any, and watched other people handing over their books to the priest to be thrown in the bonfire. That little book was destined to do a mighty work in the hearts of her family as the following paragraphs tell.

*Ned Meharg and Frank Haggerty
delivering Bibles*

*(Twenty years later a young man came to the assembly in the city of Santa Cruz. When Frank asked him: "Where do you come from?" he said: "I come from Villa Becia, an isolated village in the valleys near the Rio San Juan de Oro".*

*Frank perked up at the memory of the long trip along the River San Juan de Oro, and asked, "How did you become a believer?"*

*The young fellow answered, "When I was a boy some "gringos" came to our village and my grandmother bought a New Testament which she made me read every night. I was the only one who knew how to read in the home. Every night before going to bed I read to my grandmother and to the other family members. The words in the Book made sense to her and in time she accepted the Lord Jesus as Saviour.*

As time went on other members of the family were saved, and I also trusted the Lord".

The young man continued to tell how years later other Christians found their way into those isolated places and discovered a group of believers meeting around the Word of God. He also added, "I have come to Santa Cruz to go to study the Bible at the Hebron Seminary, and my desire is to go back and teach my people about the Lord."

Frank marvelled at the story and realized that God had brought about a wonderful harvest of saved souls. The lonely little New Testament had spoken to the people who had no other way to hear the preaching of the Gospel of Salvation.)

## Chapter 12

# MINISTERING SPIRITS (AND A DEADLY POISON)

Frank and Ned continued their travels reaching out to more villages. They arrived at a little town plaza that had a notice over a door that said, "Restaurant". It was just a dingy little room with a couple of tables and chairs, nothing impressive, but they were tired of their own cooking and decided to have a meal at the restaurant in spite of its uninviting appearance.

They went in and a woman dressed in black greeted them coolly: "Buenas tardes, what do you want?"

They said, "We would like to have a meal. Can you give us something to eat? We'll pay you for the food".

She answered, "It is past lunch time and I don't know if there is enough to cook something for you ... Let me go and ask."

She turned round and went out through a door leading to the back of the house. Soon she returned and said, "If you come back in half an hour, I will have a meal ready for you!"

Frank and Ned were pleased with the answer, delighted with the idea of some "good home cooking", and went out to scout the village a bit more, handing out tracts. When the thirty minutes were up, they returned to the restaurant where they were met by the same woman in the black dress who directed them to a table, invited them to sit down, and she said she would go and get their meal.

They were quite surprised with the change in her demeanour. She was much friendlier than before. What had happened?

The food turned out to be not so appetizing, but since hunger is a good sauce, they applied their knife and fork to the job of eating some cooked rice, potatoes and a piece of fried meat. Frank discovered his meat was a piece of lung and he found it very distasteful. But Ned being Australian was a meat eater, and ate Frank's portion along with his own. Both ordered bottles of soda and drank them to quench their thirst. Ned suddenly exclaimed, "Frank, I am terribly thirsty, give me the rest of your pop." He drained the second bottle and was still thirsty.

After paying for the meal, they left the place and went out. Ned began to feel unwell, and still complaining of terrible thirst, both went out of the village to an area by the river where they stopped, tethered their mules and got ready to camp in the open field.

Ned started having cramps and vomited till he was exhausted. Frank decided to stay overnight in the place because Ned was unable to move any further. Throughout the night he continued vomiting and was getting weaker and weaker. Frank noticed the vomit was glowing in the moonlight and he wondered what caused it to glow. He felt it was the food in the "restaurant" that didn't agree with Ned, but what to do in the open country?

Ned was delirious and he kept saying, "Frank, I am going to

die". Frank could not accept that and kept trying to encourage Ned to hold on. Ned kept saying, "I am going to die, Frank, I want my Bible to be sent to my Dad. Please."

Frank said, "Ned, you are not going to die. You have to hold on. But Ned, I will take the Bible to your Dad. I will go to Australia if the Lord takes you Home, now or later. But, Ned, you are not going to die. There is a lot of work yet to be done for the furtherance of the Gospel in this country."

Frank kept on watch between praying and trying to comfort Ned. The night passed and the light of dawn began to show on the horizon. As the sun rose, Frank could see that Ned was getting weaker, and he felt helpless in the open field, away from any possibility of help, and unable to go to the village to seek for help because Ned was too weak to be moved. He was intensely concentrated as he bowed down in supplication for his dear friend.

Suddenly, he became aware of a person standing beside him with an interested look on his face. After the customary greeting, the newcomer asked, "What is wrong with your friend?"

Frank answered and said, "My friend is very sick and has been vomiting all night. He is very weak. We are waiting here till he gets a little stronger and we can go and look for some medicine for him." The man nodded his head, turned round, and went away. Frank was puzzled by the man's attitude, his concern about Ned and his sudden departure.

Not much later, the same man returned bringing an earthen pot. Coming close to Frank, he said, "Give this to your friend." Again, without any explanation he went away, leaving Frank startled and speechless at the sudden departure.

Bending down to look at the pot, he saw it contained about three litres of milk. Frank decided to follow the man's advice, but felt it was necessary to boil the milk to avoid the possibility of making Ned worse under the circumstances. He brought a half cup of the warm milk and tried to get Ned to drink it. Ned refused, so Frank had to put the cup down to his lips and force Ned to swallow the milk. However, as soon as the milk went down, Ned again had a violent bout of vomiting and fell limp on his back. Frank got scared wondering if he had killed his dear friend, but after a short while, Ned said, "Frank, my stomach is not burning as much now."

Frank boiled more milk and cooled it in the river, brought it to Ned, and this time he didn't need to force it down his throat. Ned drank it readily because it eased the fire in his stomach. Bit by bit Frank continued giving him the milk until it was finished. Ned lapsed into a restful sleep for a few hours.

When he woke up, he was looking better, and said he was feeling better. Both decided to camp in the place for a while longer to allow Ned to grow stronger. They also realized the Lord had intervened to save Ned's life, and were praising Him for His wonderful delivery.

Frank kept waiting for the man to return to pick up his clay pot. Out in the country the people were very careful with their utensils, because these were difficult to get in those days. Money was also very scarce. Before leaving the camp site, he decided to leave the clay pot in the same place, but he put a little bit of money under it to reward the man for his kindness.

As Ned was stronger, both returned to the village, and made

a point of going past the "restaurant" where they had eaten the meal. As they walked slowly past the door, looking inside, they saw the woman in the black dress. She gave them a startled look of horror and quickly disappeared into the back of the house.

This reaction made them realize that something had been done to injure them. Walking around they also noticed that the "restaurant" was adjacent to the Roman Catholic Church. Definitely something to ponder.

Who was the man with the clay pot and the timely provision of milk? Why was he interested and friendly, different from the people in the village who were wary of the "Protestants"? They went around trying to find the man with the clay pot. They asked people if they knew who had fresh milk available, but the people answered, "There are no milking cows in this area. We only have sheep and goats".

The mystery of the man with the clay pot and the provision of milk wasn't solved in spite of their asking around. Ned and Frank's question of: "Who was the man with the clay pot?" remained without answer in their minds.

After that, they felt it was time to start on the way back home. Ned was still quite weak and it wasn't wise to press further on. After twenty-six days away they returned to Tupiza, feeling they had accomplished the mission of taking the Gospel of the Lord Jesus Christ to people who had never heard it before.

As they continued to travel around, they met other missionaries, Dr. Roger Brown among them. Dr. Brown had felt called to work among the Quechua people and had lived in a Quechua hut for a fairly long time. This enabled him to learn their language very well, and he was able to help in the translation of the New Testament which became a great tool to reach Quechuas with the Gospel.

Roger Brown had a good knowledge of the customs and culture in the country areas. He was interested to hear the report about the trip to the River San Juan de Oro, and to hear about their experiences. He listened very carefully to the story of Ned's illness, the intense thirst, the phosphorescent vomiting and the story of the milk in the clay pot. Being a medical man, he was able to analyse the symptoms they described and came to the conclusion they had been given rat poison, hence the intense thirst. The vomiting had helped but what really saved Ned was the milk. Roger Brown said it must have been goat's milk which is the best antidote known for rat poison.

He also told them that certain women made a vow to serve the priests in the church in whatever service was asked of them. Proof of their vow was to wear black clothes to demonstrate their devotion. This used to be a prevalent custom in the little towns and villages from colonial times.

No doubt she went to consult with the priest regarding the "Protestants" who were looking for a meal. No need for further speculation! No wonder the woman in the black dress reacted with such horror when she saw her victims look inside her restaurant. Was she wondering if they had come to remonstrate with her?

Why wasn't Frank affected in the same way as Ned? The poison must have been in the meat. Frank didn't eat the meat but Ned ate a double portion of it.

Who was the man with the clay pot and the timely provision

of goat's milk? Had they been visited by an angelic messenger from God in the time of their greatest need? Frank believed without a shadow of doubt that the man was an angel come from God, as in Hebrews 1 verse 14. Why did the Lord give this remarkable answer to prayer? Perhaps because Ned became a true pioneer for the Gospel, opening areas and starting churches in inhospitable places. He and his wife Flora travelled along the rivers in the Northern part of Bolivia, and reached many, many souls for the Lord.

The Lord knew the value of this man, who though he found it difficult to learn the language had persevered. He was a rough diamond, as Frank used to call him with affection, but also a dedicated servant who was going to bring honour and glory to God in his devotion and service. God omniscient sent an angelic minister to bring the right antidote to the poison. Only God knew His servant Ned would become a great pioneer in the Lord's work in Bolivia.

*Chapter 13*

# THE NEXT CHAPTER

After Ned regained his strength, the two friends continued travelling around the country areas, visiting different places, always seeking to preach the Gospel to everyone they met. Their friendship became stronger as they shared experiences in their service for the Lord. Both were earnestly seeking the Lord's guidance as to the places the Lord would have them work.

Ned and Frank continued their travels evangelizing in the country areas. They travelled in the Altiplano. Later they found their way by jeep to the eastern part of Bolivia, visiting the Gran Chaco region, where Ned found the hot dry climate very agreeable to his Australian taste and upbringing!

In those years the roads in Bolivia were dirt roads, full of pot holes, sand traps in the dry season, and miry bogs in the rain. A driver had to have a knowledge of mechanics, carry a good supply of spare parts and extra gasoline, apart from a good supply of water and food stuffs as often they travelled long stretches without seeing any houses or places where they could buy supplies. Truckers went in convoys to help each other out of the deep ruts in the roads and shared spare parts as trucks broke down due to the terrible road conditions. They named a very trying area of that road "La Gloria" to get a laugh. It was anything but Glorious!

In those years the unwritten law of the road was to help any cars or trucks that were stuck or broken down by the roadside. Gasoline was shared at no cost from the spare cans with the instruction to share it with another needy driver. Ned and Frank often joined those convoys, and at night the truckers would camp out and they wanted to hear the stories the "gringos" had to tell them. In that way a number of truckers heard the Gospel message around the campfire.

The men and their helpers always slept on top of their trucks to keep themselves safe from wild beasts. They advised Frank and Ned to do the same, to sleep inside the Land Rover or on top of one of the trucks for safety. On a particular night, they again reminded the "gringos" of the danger, but both friends decided they would be more comfortable stretching out in their little tent.

They were told to be afraid of tigers in that region, but Ned and Frank thought the truckers were teasing them. They went to sleep in their tent as usual, tired after the arduous trek of the day. Early the next day, the men came and shouted, "Hey, you gringos, wake up! Come and see!"

Frank and Ned left the tent and the men showed them tiger tracks, as big as a man's hand, about ten feet away from the tent. They could hardly believe their eyes. Apparently, the tiger passed near the tent, but continued on his prowl without bothering the sleepers. The truckers were amazed, since quite often stories were told of people being attacked and maimed by tigers or mountain lions.

Frank and Ned realized that the Angel of the Lord must have kept watch over their tent that night, and they decided to be more cautious in their travels. They also agreed that it was wise to listen to the advice of the experienced Bolivian drivers.

But the time had come for the deep friends to move and settle into their calling. Frank returned to Santa Cruz, ready to begin the next chapter in his missionary adventure.

Ned returned to visit Dr. Roger Brown, whose old Studebaker was needing a lot of work in order to be able to continue his travels in the Alkatuyo region with the Gospel. Ned was an excellent mechanic and offered his services. Ned went to work on the truck, and there met Miss Flora Levy who was then newly arrived in Bolivia. His next chapter was about to begin.

## Chapter 14

# FLORA (née LEVY) MEHARG

"The Lord gathers His servants out of the lands. From the East and from the West ... From the North and from the South" (Psalm 107:3).

This wonderful truth is reflected in the lives of men and women who go out as missionaries to serve the Lord. They have the same vision of taking the message of salvation to the people of the country, to teach them to walk in newness of life enjoying peace with God, forgiveness of sin, and the fellowship of the Church. When they meet one another the missionary family become very tightly knit despite their differing countries of origin as they share life in a foreign country and often help one another as needs arise.

In the land of Palestine, in the old city of Jerusalem, a Jewish couple welcomed their new baby girl to the family and they called her Flora. They were a couple who loved the Lord Jehovah and brought up their children to be very obedient to the practices of the religious life of the synagogue. Their children were sent to the British school, but after a time, they had to find other schools since the British School was expensive and Mr. & Mrs. Levy could no longer afford to keep them all in the same school.

Flora, being the youngest, was sent to the Christian School, even though she hated the Jesus of the Christians. As she went, she met the principal, Miss Clark, who from the beginning told the students the Christian story seeking to instruct them in the knowledge of the Lord Jesus.

Flora rebelled against the teaching and vowed in her heart that she would not listen to any teaching about the man Jesus, much less change her religion. In truth, she was hard on the girls who were sympathetic to the Christian staff and their faith. As time went on, however, and she listened to the New Testament accounts, she began to feel a sympathetic softness in her heart toward the sufferings that Jesus had to go through. She realized He had been a good man and His teachings were good, but she was not ready to accept His claim to be the Messiah.

As more time went on, she had to make a decision about her further education. No longer could she plan, as she had intended, to go to France due to rumours of war, so she decided to start nurse's training at the Hadassah Hospital in Jerusalem. Throughout this period, she continued reading her Bible, and kept her friendship with Miss Clark who, in turn, continued to tell her about the Lord Jesus.

The spiritual struggle continued to trouble Flora. She wanted to remain loyal to the Jewish faith she had learned from childhood, but at the same time she was terribly disturbed in her spirit.

One night in the quietness of her bedroom she knelt and cried from her heart, "God Jehovah, God of Abraham, Isaac and Jacob, I want to remain faithful to You, but please reveal to me if Jesus of Nazareth is the Messiah". Peace and happiness flooded her soul that night and she thanked God for the confirmation she had received in answer to her prayer and for the peace she enjoyed as it was confirmed to her that the man Jesus was indeed the Promised Messiah.

She continued reading her Christian Bible, but her family were getting suspicious of her interest in it and took it away from her. Flora still had a small New Testament and read it continually, feeding her soul and growing in the faith. She started attending the Christian Church which Miss Clark attended. Eventually she decided to take the step of baptism, and she told her family.

As expected, her family were completely shocked at their daughter's confession of faith and pronounced her dead to the family and said Kadish for her. Though no longer welcome at home, God sent a wonderful and timely provision for Flora, and she was invited to stay with a Christian couple while a lady missionary was absent on furlough. She continued her nursing studies at the hospital in Jerusalem. It was sad to feel the estrangement from her dear family, but she learned that her mother would come from time to time to the hospital to inquire about Flora and this knowledge gave her a warm feeling.

One day Miss Clark visited Flora and said: "Flora, our school is connected with a teaching hospital in London. Would you like to go to there to continue your training?" Flora felt she saw the heavens open, and she was enchanted by the idea of having her own room and freedom to study her Bible without any opposition, as well as being able to continue her nursing training. (Later she became an accomplished midwife.)

While living in London, Flora was able to find an assembly that welcomed her into their fellowship and helped her in her

Christian life and development. At the same time, she was exposed to contacts with missionaries who often came to London on their way home on furlough, or going abroad to their sphere of service.

Flora remembered that as a child her great desire had been to go as a missionary to speak to people about God. Now that she had found the Saviour, the Lord Jesus, that desire re-awakened and she started  looking for direction to a field of service where she could use her nursing skills and witness for the Lord.

As time went on, she heard many reports about missionary work in different countries. Being a girl she was afraid to consider going to a country that could be threatening to single girls. Some godly people encouraged her just to trust the Lord to take her to the place where she would be used best.

A letter from Dr. Roger Brown was sent to the assembly in London giving a report of the work in and around Alkatuyo. He mentioned the medical work in the little clinic he had in his home and also mentioned how many Quechua Indians needed medical care. Often he found himself swamped with the medical needs on top of the evangelism he engaged in travelling to  visit the market fairs.

Flora felt that this was the door opening for her. She would join Roger and Adell Brown who would be good companions. In addition, she would be in a "protected" area. She was commended by the assembly in London to the Lord's work in Bolivia, and in 1951 she sailed for Bolivia toward a new life of service.

## Chapter 15

# CHANGING RINGS IN ALKATUYO

So it was that in 1951 Flora Levy arrived in Potosi. She was met by the Browns and went with them to Alkatuyo where she was slowly introduced to the work of preaching the Gospel to the Quechua people as well as giving some medical and nursing care. Dr. Brown ran a small clinic in his home to give medical care to sick folk who would come in asking for his aid. This work was a big help for the poor Quechua peasants who had no access to any medical facilities in the country areas. Those were very hard times for the people out in the country who had to survive with little support.

Alkatuyo is a rural area in the Andean plateau of Potosi. There is no real town apart from the central school where the children gathered from the scattered Quechua huts that dotted the countryside. People eked out a living by growing what they could in the short Andean growing season. Where possible, they also kept sheep, chickens and llamas.

*(Later when Frank and I worked in Alkatuyo while the Browns were on furlough, we became very aware of the need for medical training to*

*help in poor country areas. Hardly a week passed by without people coming in with desperate emergencies. For example, on one occasion a poor man came with a hand blown off by a stick of dynamite he was handling in one of their feasts. During that period, Frank regretted not going to the Missionary School of Medicine in London, before he left for Bolivia. I, Blanquita, regretted not having been able to study nursing.)*

The evangelistic work at that time was carried out by travelling to the different areas where the Quechua people would hold open air markets to trade their goods and produce. Money wasn't used at the fairs, since people depended on bartering to trade for all their needs, a practice carried on from ancient times. The best dates for the market fairs were also the feast days for Saints in the Roman Catholic calendar. The markets moved from village to village.

On market days, Dr. Brown started the day at the crack of dawn and travelled to the fair accompanied by some Quechua believers who had come to faith and also desired to testify of their faith to other Quechuas. They went to the market and spent time among the people, speaking to them, giving out tracts and selling Scriptures. Dr. Brown was fluent in the Quechua language and that helped him to communicate the message of the Gospel.

However, by 10-11 am, the people would begin to drink "chicha", a type of maize beer with a high alcohol content. It was freely imbibed by men and women, and by midday many were no longer sober. They became aggressive, and particularly angry with outsiders. Missionaries were targeted, often incited by a visiting or local priest who set the people against the evangelical missionaries. The missionaries and Quechua believers had to be very cautious not to stay on past this stage, and they cleared out before it became too dangerous for them.

The reliability of Dr. Brown's Studebaker was integral to the missionary work! So, Ned's arrival and mechanical know-how was very welcome. Shortly after his arrival, Ned wrote Frank in Santa Cruz, telling him that he was "changing the rings" in the engine. Frank wrote back telling Ned to beware of changing rings with the lively and attractive Jewish girl! He had met Flora Levy at a gathering for missionary candidates in Wales before he left for Bolivia and knew she was very friendly and attractive.

Another letter followed soon after, saying that Ned was again "changing rings" but this time it was an engagement ring that Ned was giving Flora! He had found the helpmeet to share his life and passion for the Lord's work in Bolivia.

(*Ned's engagement to Flora marked a turning point for both Frank and Ned, not only personally, but also in the discernment of the direction of each one's future work in Bolivia. The grand adventures of travelling together to share the Scriptures and the Gospel in far-flung settlements had been wonderful and very formative, but it was now time to rise to the challenge of investing in a specific place and task. Ned travelled to various places in the country, trying to discern where the Lord was preparing the place where he and Flora should labour.*

*Little could I have guessed that Ned and Flora's engagement would have such an impact on my own life, nor that Frank and I would marry before they did! But that story is for a later chapter.*)

## Chapter 16

# RELIGIOUS FREEDOM

Missionaries working among the Quechua and Aymara people found the work very hard going. There were many obstacles to the Gospel including the age-old custom of obligatory Community Work as well as the patriarchal Control of families. In addition, they had to deal with entrenched superstition, animism, and witchcraft from the traditional pagan religions, despite a veneer of Christianity. There was also the strong opposition from the Roman Catholic Church against Protestants ("evangélicos"), expressed across all sectors of society. Both the overt opposition from the Roman Catholic institution and the more covert resistance from indigenous religions were tied closely together for historical reasons.

When the Spanish conquered the land that is now Bolivia in 1535, they were accompanied by Dominican priests and the successful 'discovery' of the new world was seen as a blessing by God. The land was decreed to belong to Spain by Charles V of Spain. The Spanish crown rewarded those who had "discovered" the land with an "ecomienda" - a colonial practice imported from Spain in which a portion of land and the people living and working it were entrusted to an encomendero. The obligations of encomendero were to protect, educate, and Christianise the people. Although couched in benign terms, in practice, it involved enslaving people and expropriating their lands. This system of encomiendas was made easier by the fact that the peoples in the region were previously under the Inca Empire, which had established systems of tribute and obligatory communal labour as well as slavery. (Indeed, when the system of encomiendas was abolished legally, these became the landed estates, or "haciendas" complete with indentured peons that Frank and Ned encountered in their travels to distant villages.)

The role of the Roman Catholic Church in the conquest was complex, with some priests working to limit abuses of the Indigenous people, advocate successfully for the abolition of encomiendas and function as missionaries. But for the most part, the institution aligned itself closely with the conquistadors and the Spanish Crown. For most Bolivians the Spanish conquest and the Roman Catholic Church go hand in hand. Large tracts of land were allocated by Spain to the Catholic Church, and like in Europe, bishoprics were at the heart of secular as well as religious governance.

The practice of slavery, tributes and forced communal labour became particularly indispensable when large deposits of silver and gold were discovered in the Bolivian mountain of Potosi in 1544. The slave and forced communal labour in the mines of Potosi financed much of the Spanish Empire and the Counter-reformation in Europe for the next 100 years. Conditions were so harsh in the mines that it is estimated that as much as 50% of the Indigenous Andean population was decimated.

The "Christianisation" of the Indigenous population was accomplished not only through measures such as obligatory attendance at mass in the encomiendas, but also through incorporation of many of the laws, practices and beliefs of the Indigenous religions into the local version of Roman Catholicism. So, a god such as Pacha Mama, Mother Earth, was closely associated with the Virgin Mary, and festivals of gods were renamed by coinciding saints' days. So the solstice festival of the sun god, Inti Raymi, is conflated with the saint's day of John the Baptist. The Roman Catholic Church had virtually total control over religious affairs in Bolivia.

When Bolivia achieved its independence from Spain in 1826, its constitution stated that the Apostolic Roman Catholic faith was the religion of the new republic to the exclusion of every other public form of worship. Under the strong influence of Simon Bolivar, this article was followed by a statement that the state respects and recognizes the principle that no human power has authority over individual conscience.

So Protestant and Evangelical missionaries in the early 20th Century found a country in the grip of the Roman Catholic Church, where they were not welcome. Anything new in religious practice was labelled as Protestant, demonic, and from hell. Public gatherings by evangelical believers were particularly risky. Consequently, missionaries had a very hard task to break new ground. They were often attacked physically and their homes or places of worship burned, often incited by Roman Catholic priests. But some of the earliest believers in Bolivia were lawyers, and they engaged in courageous legal defence of the missionaries who faced criminal charges of public practice of a non-Roman Catholic faith. In particular, the defence of the Irish missionary, William Payne, in the highest court made the case that the principle of respect for individual conscience could not exclude public expression of that faith. So in 1906 the Bolivian Constitution was amended to: "The state recognizes and supports the Apostolic Roman Catholic religion, but permits public practice of all other faiths".

Despite this achievement, well into the 20th Century the preaching of salvation by faith alone was opposed - often violently - by the Roman Catholic establishment. Even the distribution of Bibles was problematic since Bible reading by lay people was discouraged actively before the 2nd Vatican Council in 1962. That is why the Bibles that Ned and Frank sold were often confiscated and burned publicly by the Catholic priests in the villages they visited. That is why good Catholics could resort to often violent means to protect their own faith.

The Indigenous and serving class, especially, were also gripped by their traditional superstitions, often masked under the cloak of the Roman Catholic religion. Throughout the years on festival days the priests performed their Catholic rites early in the day with their church members. However, as the day progressed and especially as the Indigenous people got under the influence of alcohol, they reverted to the old pagan ways, for example, offering sacrifices to Pacha Mama, the Earth goddess.

(*Some years later, when Frank and I were serving in Uyuni, Frank and a companion, Crispin, were returning from an evangelistic trip across the Salt Lake of Uyuni, when they saw a bright fire burning in the night. During those years the unwritten law of the country for any traveller was to draw near and check up on the situation to offer help if needed since people sometimes got stranded in the Salt Lake and died of exposure because of the intense Andean cold.*

*Naturally Crispin and Frank went to investigate and found a group gathered around the body of a newly-killed llama near the fire. He recognized some of the people as professionals from the town of Uyuni, well-known neighbours, so he wanted to offer help. He was quite surprised to feel Crispin tugging his arm urgently and pleading with him to turn back and disappear from the place before being seen by the others. Frank allowed Crispin to lead him back to the vehicle, puzzled at seeing those educated people in that situation and the urgency in his companion's voice.*

*As they went on their way home, Crispin explained to Frank that those people were in the process of offering an animal sacrifice to the Pacha Mama, hoping to get blessing and prosperity in their business.*

*"But those people are Roman Catholics", Frank exclaimed, still not understanding what he had seen, "I have seen them in the processions, and also entering the Catholic Church!"*

*Patiently Crispin explained that both Indigenous and European-descended professional people who were practising Roman Catholics, were not averse to help fate by practising the ancient pagan rites.)*

The reforms introduced by the Government in the 1950s not only changed the face of the country, but also created new opportunities for missionary work. The overt and covert religious opposition to the Gospel remained but Ned and Frank were also starting their missionary work at the changing of the tide.

The Educational reform not only developed literacy but also made the New Testament widely available. There followed a mighty work of the Holy Spirit among the Indigenous people from the Bolivian Andean plateau. Many turned to the Lord, resulting in the founding of many assemblies in the country areas.

The new believers wanted to share their faith with neighbours near and far.

The Agrarian reform added an interesting angle to the spread of the Gospel. Many people from the Altiplano relocated to the lowlands to farm a portion of land that had been allocated by the Government. They were truly immigrants and settlers in a new land and new climate! The internal migration from the Andean plateau to the lowlands also broke the pre-Conquest yoke of patriarchal control and community dues, which had set the stage for the serf-like conditions that became the norm for the semi-feudal land estates. The patriarchal communal system was also strongly tied to vows and rites to Mother Earth (Pacha Mama).

The new settlers were open to the Word of God. Several were already believers before they came to the lowlands, and some felt the call to come and witness to the immigrant settlers as "tentmakers". As a result, there was a big movement among the settlers to accept the message of the Gospel. After the first crops were gathered, the new believers went back to their homeland to visit their parents, taking produce from their new land. Many also took the opportunity to give a good report of how the Lord had blessed them. The old folks listened quietly to their stories and testimonies of God's work in their lives. Their sons and daughters were no longer under them but they still acted honourably toward the old folks as the Scriptures had taught them. This made an impact on the older generation and many decided to accept the Lord Jesus as Saviour.

## Chapter 17

# SEEDS IN HARD GROUND

The grip of the Roman Catholic Church meant that missionaries had a very hard task to break new ground. That was particularly true among the European-descended class whose position of privilege with the Spanish conquest was linked tightly to religious participation in the Roman Catholic Church. However, even this hard ground could be softened by the lives of missionaries and their message of salvation through faith alone in the life, death and resurrection of the Lord Jesus Christ.

One of the pioneer missionaries was Dr. George Hamilton, commended from New Zealand assemblies. When he came to Bolivia in 1911, he revalidated his medical qualification. If he wasn't appreciated as an evangelical missionary, his work as a medical doctor was, and this opened doors to reach people with the Gospel message. The Hamiltons moved from Sucre and Potosi to Santa Cruz in 1921. They replaced the courageous missionary, Will Payne, whose consistent challenge to criminal charges of public promotion of a faith other than Roman Catholicism had spearheaded the granting of Religious Freedom ("Libertad de Culto") to the Bolivian people.

In Santa Cruz, they found the familiar opposition, but were

accepted by the local residents because of Dr. Hamilton's medical profession. A foreign doctor who was willing to help everybody also created a feeling of jealousy among the other medical practitioners in the city. However, a critical incident established his reputation as an excellent doctor and a generous colleague, and this gave many opportunities to speak the Gospel message.

A man needed surgery and Dr. Hamilton proposed a procedure that was contrary to the surgery and treatment proposed by local doctors. Dr. Hamilton was convinced that their proposal could mean possible death to the patient. Dr. Hamilton knew that if he followed their advice, he could be accused of malpractice and even manslaughter, so he arranged for his surgical procedure to be witnessed by the doctors and by the British Ambassador to ensure transparency. The success of the event to the wellbeing of the patient opened the way for more interaction with the medical profession and increased his scope of influence into the highest strata of society.

His medical reputation brought him into contact with a young woman and daughter of a well-to-do family, Blanca Montero Oyos. A bad fall from a horse had injured her knee and she was in danger of totally losing movement in the joint. Dr. Hamilton's treatment was able to save the knee from immobility. This began a friendly relationship with the family. He witnessed faithfully to the young woman about salvation by faith in the Lord Jesus, but though it never seemed to register with her or her family, the warm relationship softened their hearts toward Protestant missionaries.

This benefitted the next missionary couple, Mr. & Mrs. Peter Horne, who arrived in Santa Cruz to replace the Hamiltons in in 1928. The Hornes could not find a house to rent because of the religious opposition, so the Montero Oyos family invited the couple to move into their very large house, where the Hornes stayed for a couple of years. Despite this openness to the missionaries, the Gospel message was ignored at that time. The father, Sixto Montero, died suddenly in his sleep of a cardiac arrest during a siesta. It is believed by many that he had accepted the Lord quietly some time before.

(*It is important to remember that religious affiliation was decided for a family than by individuals at the time. Overt acceptance of the Gospel presented by missionaries implied a rejection of Roman Catholicism to become Protestant - not only for the head of the family but also for the whole household. This would be accompanied by exclusion from the privileges and access to power that came with the religious participation in baptisms, weddings, funerals and feast days that were at the centre of society life for the ruling class.*)

In 1929, Blanca Montero married Ernesto Weise, an electrical engineer and member of a prominent family of European-trained professionals. A baby girl was born to the young couple and named after the mother, Blanquita ("little Blanca). The baby was precocious and her good progress made the young couple very happy. Like parents everywhere, they delighted to watch the first steps of their nine-month old baby girl.

However, one day they noticed a little limp: Baby Blanquita was having difficulty controlling the use of one leg. They hoped that after a few days everything would be normal again, but the limp became worse, and after a few weeks they noticed their baby was behaving as though she was suffering pain. The little one refused to stand and could not use her legs as before. The baby cried sorely with any moving of the knee joints.

Visits to doctors started but there was no clear diagnosis. Polio was suggested, since the daughter of friends had been diagnosed with polio. But that did not fit. Arthritis was proposed, but who had heard of arthritis in an infant? And there was no history of arthritis in the family. But Infantile Rheumatoid Arthritis was the final diagnosis.

The child received all the care possible at the time, but she became quite crippled. However, when a second baby girl was welcomed into the family and started to take her first steps, Blanquita also started learning again to walk with her sister. Everybody was more than happy to see this. But episodes of crippling Inflammatory Arthritis would continue to recur.

The spiritual trajectory of the family was changed by two tragedies. In 1935, when Blanquita was 5 years old, the beloved brother of Blanca, Constantino Montero, was brutally murdered. As a recently-trained civil engineer, he was engaged by the government to survey land to plan the opening of new roads that would connect the country and promote economic growth. He was surveying in the traditional territory of the Guarayu people. The installation of roads was firmly opposed by the priests who had established Guarayu reservations ("reducciones") and wanted them to remain isolated. Constantino and his party of Guarayu guides were confronted by other Guarayu who had been ordered by the priest to kill the engineer, who was decapitated and his body thrown in the river. The Guarayu guides were ostensibly spared but were later poisoned so that the story would not circulate. Two of the guides, however, survived and after three months arrived in Santa Cruz with the sad news. The priest in question was charged and convicted, but "escaped" mysteriously the day before his execution. This led to Mother Blanca's loss of faith and rejection of Christianity. She famously threw all her statues of saints on the floor and refused to attend any event associated with the Church.

Later, the family moved to the country to try their hand at farming. In 1942, an accidental fire, that burned their home down, left the young family of seven children destitute and homeless. This event was interpreted as divine judgment for having rejected the Roman Catholic faith, especially by Ernesto's emphatically Catholic mother. So to the loss was added the injury of social judgment and exclusion. The Horne missionaries, who had received hospitality from Blanca's parents, faithfully came to visit, bringing what little they could share at the time, (this happened during the Second World War). They also brought the message of the love of God. Blanca finally yielded her heart to the Lord, finding peace and release from the depression that had plagued her since her beloved brother's death. Eventually her husband, Ernesto, also became a believer and the whole family became associated with the evangelical faith.

(*It is amazing to see God's patience and persistence over many years, lovingly seeking the "lost sheep". The seeds of consistent kindness and proclamation of the Gospel by missionaries bore fruit even in the hard ground of a society in the grip of privilege and the Roman Catholic Church. The seed bore fruit, small at first, but as we shall see yielding thirtyfold, sixtyfold and a hundredfold.*)

*Chapter 18*

# BLANQUITA

While Frank was growing up and coming to faith in Scotland, I - Blanquita - was growing up and coming to faith in the far-off land of Bolivia in the small sandy, tropical town of Santa Cruz.

My young life was punctuated by bouts of Inflammatory Arthritis that reappeared without warning, affecting more joints, especially hands, wrists, knees, ankles and feet. These episodes were followed by yet another time of being confined to bed or to a chair. Wisely, Mother Blanca taught me to read at an early age so that I could entertain myself while my siblings were out playing.

The loss of the family home and turn in our fortunes happened when I was 11 years old. The fire started on the thatched roof, and once it reached the nearby room where fuel was stored for machinery and ammunition for hunting, it exploded and spread rapidly. It happened during siesta time and we got out of the house with only what we were wearing during siesta. Everything, everything else burned. I vividly remember watching the devastation: Father in his siesta pyjamas and slippers; Mother in her house dress with two-month old Betty in her arms. Most of us did not have shoes on. It was a shocked and mournful ride by oxcart to my mother's big childhood house and to my maternal grandmother, Manuela, who took in the ragged family of seven children. It was a very difficult time. Many in the extended family censured us, citing this as proof of God's judgment for leaving the Catholic Church, but others were kind and generous, helping us slowly recover some of what we had lost, and hosting different children for extended periods to ease the burden on Grandmother. After a year, my father Ernesto's family gave us their country house, just outside the town, as our new place to live. (It was actually a bowling alley Grandfather had built to entertain friends and family!)

Mother suffered this second loss acutely and she found it difficult to manage. As the eldest, I dropped out of school to assume the responsibility of caring for my six siblings. As someone who had learned to read early, I had loved school and relished learning, so stopping my education was very difficult, and a wound and regret I carried my whole life.

My typical day started early at 6am by going to the market to buy the meat and other food for the day - a necessity in our hot climate and without the benefit of refrigeration at home. On returning there was always a lot to do to keep the house clean and get the main meal prepared for midday. The boys went to school in the morning (so girls could help with tasks at home!); and the girls in the afternoon, so helping brothers and sisters get to school seemed constant! The conditions in the country house were basic to say the least! Water needed to be brought from the well and the house constantly swept clean of the sand and dust that blew through the windows that had shutters but no screens or glass. Tasks got easier when Father installed a hand pump to bring water from the well into the kitchen!

Father was a founding member of the local electrical cooperative, which was setting up electricity in the city (we were early beneficiaries!) and slowly we recovered to a modest economic level and to our place in society. But when I was a teenager I had three life-changing experiences, that changed my pathway.

*First.* The first happened as a young teenager one Wednesday night when I accompanied Mother to the Gospel Hall. The message was on "The Ten Virgins of Matthew 25." As I listened to the preacher, I realized I was in the same position as the Foolish Virgins. I was convicted in my soul about being left out of the Marriage Feast and heading to an eternity in hell. I spent the next few days in terror of dying before I had a chance to speak with someone about how to get the 'Oil of Salvation'. I knew I was at hell's door and felt that a decision had to be made now or I would be forever lost. I kept praying, "Lord, don't let me die without salvation."

The following Sunday, when I went to Sunday School, I asked help from the missionary, who explained the way of salvation by trusting the Lord Jesus as Saviour. I went home rejoicing in the fact that now I had acquired the precious gift of salvation and no matter what came afterwards, the door of Heaven would never be closed for me.

(*That experience led me in later years to teach clearly the need to trust in the Lord Jesus Christ while we live, because a second after death, it becomes too late. Thus, I taught my children the message of salvation by faith placed in the Lord Jesus Christ as the only way to Heaven. I did not want my precious children to become firebrands in hell! That conviction was always at the front of my mind as I explained the Gospel message to others.*)

At fifteen years of age a group of teenagers were asking for baptism, and I wanted to join them. But my father wisely advised me to wait until I was more mature and certain of the seriousness of my commitment. I was baptized at seventeen, and soon after invited to be a Sunday School teacher for the little ones. It was there I had my second life-changing experience.

*Second.* One Sunday at the end of teaching the lesson to my class of children in Sunday School, one little girl chirped: "Señorita, today is my birthday, I am eight years old." I congratulated her: "Happy birthday, Maria!" thinking that was the end of the matter.

Maria again spoke, "Señorita, I also want to accept Jesus as my Saviour today!"

In fear and trembling I explained how to be saved by trusting Jesus as personal Saviour. Maria took the step of salvation and went home a happy little girl.

I had experienced the good described in James 5 verse 20: "The one who turns a sinner from the error of his way will save a soul from death and cover a multitude of sins." The experience of leading little Maria to the joy of full salvation seeded a "missionary vision" to reach souls and rescue them from death and sin. I began praying, exploring in my mind and spirit how to become a missionary. It was a quiet exercise of heart between the Lord and me, waiting on God to lead the way. I only knew of foreign missionaries and could not imagine how this vision would materialize. I knew it had to come directly from God. He would show the sphere of work and would provide for daily needs.

I engaged in all the activities in the assembly, a natural thing for someone who desires to serve the Lord. Being shy, I was reluctant to speak in public. Once in a women's meeting, I was shaking when asked to give my testimony and tell of my conversion. When the meeting was finished I came out hanging on to my girlfriend's arm and saying, "Never again ... never, never, never again!" Sometimes I imagine how the Lord has to smile at things we say for He knew His plans for my life.

*Third*. The third life-changing experience happened at age eighteen years. After some years of good health, the dreaded Inflammatory Arthritis returned, this time for many months. I became once again completely crippled, every activity had to be dropped. and I was confined to bed. I became a sad sight - just skin and bones. I needed to be carried from place to place. At the worst of the crisis, for a period of a full month, I even had to be fed all my meals because I could not hold a fork or spoon.

*Blanquita single*

Once again, my love of reading helped me cope. I scoured the Bible where I found help to continue. One day, finding myself especially touched by God's presence, I responded in a heartfelt prayer from the bottom of my soul that I would give over my whole life to be used in God's service: for my whole life if He gave healing, or to be taken to the joy of His Presence, if not. Very soon after, the inflamed joints started to improve. I was slowly returning to movement. Some days later I told my mother, "I have a feeling that this problem is going to get better." Mother almost shouted "Amen!".

It had been a dreadful year of stress and pain and medical expenses. Slowly but surely, healthy movement returned to the joints and I was returning to a normal life. I went to Brazil for several months to get more medical help, and also to visit relatives. After learning to speak Portuguese almost fluently in just a matter of months, I discovered I had a gift for languages, including a rediscovery and deep appreciation for my own language of Spanish.

I returned from the trip to Brazil with a new perspective and a new way of seeing the world. My family even noticed that I spoke Spanish differently! In the assembly it was decided to make a joint Welcome Home party for fully recovered Sunday School teacher, and for the new missionary, Frank Haggerty, who had arrived in Santa Cruz the day after I did to join Mr. and Mrs. Peter Horne!

## Chapter 19

# MARIA, A SOWER OF SEEDS

The experience of leading Maria to faith sowed the seed in my heart for the vision to be a missionary and extend the reach of the Gospel. More importantly, the seed of God's Word and the Holy Spirit began a palpable change in little Maria, which also sowed further seeds.

One day, Frank - who knew nothing of my experience at that point - was approached in the street by an angry man who rudely demanded to know what the "Evangelistas" had done to his little Maria. The man was don ("Mr.") Sixto Porcel, her father. What had happened? What had they done to change his Maria from a difficult kid into a pleasant and obedient child! Frank wisely invited Sixto to come to listen to the message that had caused the change in Maria's behaviour.

One Wednesday evening, Sixto sneaked into the Gospel Hall, listened well to the Gospel message, but flew out of the door before anyone could speak to him. However, the Holy Spirit was working in Sixto, who repeated the visits several times and a short while later he yielded his heart to the Lord.

Maria's mother was a staunch Roman Catholic and had suffered much from her husband's philandering and drinking.

She was furious when he mentioned his conversion to the Lord Jesus in the Protestant church. Ever since she had married Sixto, there had been a fight over the drink and his waste of money on women and other things that kept the home in poverty. For many years she had taken her burden to the priest, to the Virgin Mary, to the church. She had paid much money for masses to save him, but nothing had so far availed.

Yet now, within a short time, her husband visibly changed his ways. Don Sixto bought a Bible and started reading it daily, demanding that all the family be around the table to listen. He stopped the drinking and his other vices. He brought the children he had had with other women, and asked his wife, doña ("Mrs.") Maria, to help him care for them. Finally, he demanded that everyone should go to Sunday School with young Maria.

The change in don Sixto caused doña Maria to look seriously into the Scriptures. Eventually the testimony of his changed life spoke to her and she also trusted Christ as her Saviour. Things started to change for the family in other ways too. Don Sixto bought property to build a house in a new suburb. Doña Maria started a children's club in their house. It paved the way to begin the second assembly meeting in the city of Santa Cruz.

The children's club at the Porcel house was led by the new missionary, Frank, and the Sunday School teacher, Blanquita. Frank was still developing his language skills. His gift of story-telling engaged the children as enthusiastic and generous language teachers. I, Blanquita, played the accordion.

In a wonderful way the eight-year-old Maria became a seed and sowed other seeds. Not only had her coming to faith planted a desire in my heart to serve the Lord as a missionary, but she was the seed of the Gospel to her family. First her father, followed by her mother and then one by one, her brothers and sisters. The family home became the seed of a new assembly. Two of her sisters worked full-time with Campus Crusade.

(*After being away for several years, when I returned to the city of Santa Cruz I asked for little Maria and was saddened to learn that at one point Maria had become sick. In spite of all the medical care received, she died. But she had lived to see her alcoholic father change his life completely by trusting the Lord as Saviour, and to see her mother saved as well. Maria lived only five years as a child of God, but what a power for the Gospel! In time the entire family became a testimony to the life-changing power of the Gospel of Jesus Christ in the area where they lived.*)

## Chapter 20

# A HELPMEET FOR FRANK

Ned, having found an helpmeet for himself, now wanted his friend Frank to find one also, since the companionship they had enjoyed together in the work would come to a close after his marriage.

He came to visit Santa Cruz, to see and meet the people there while still seeking where the Lord wanted him and Flora to labour after their marriage.

One evening, Ned told Frank that it was time for him to find a helpmeet. He suggested Blanquita, the Sunday School teacher. Also, said he, if Frank felt before the Lord that she would be a helpmeet for him, then he was to go ahead and ask the question. Ned was a blunt Australian and he always went directly to the point!

Ever since my experience of leading little Maria to the joy of full salvation, I, Blanquita, had been quietly praying, exploring in my mind and spirit how to become a missionary. It was a quiet exercise of heart between the Lord and me, waiting on God to lead the way. I knew it had to come directly from God. He would show the sphere of work and would provide for daily needs.

Then one evening I went to the Mission House to study a new piece of music on the accordion. Mr. & Mrs. Horne were sitting outside on the patio enjoying the cool evening.

Frank asked me to accompany him to the dining room. He proceeded to ask the question that had been burning in his heart ever since Ned spoke to him. "Blanquita, will you marry me?"

As I heard the question, Revelation 4 verse 1 suddenly came into my mind, "I saw an open door." I knew that here was the door I had been looking for since my experience with Maria. I said "Yes" without any shadow of doubt, because I knew God had worked it out.

Mr. & Mrs. Horne were quite upset with the news. Perhaps losing their new missionary and a Sunday School teacher at the same time was hard to take!

For Frank the next hurdle was the visit to Mr. and Mrs. Weise for the traditional asking of their daughter's hand in marriage!

Mother, being a believer, was thrilled with the news of her daughter marrying in the Lord. But Father was upset. This "missionary" wanted to marry his eldest, dearest, and delicate daughter! He proceeded to ask Frank how he planned to support his wife, since he had no visible means of income, he wasn't employed, he had no salary. Frank explained about his commendation to be a missionary and that he lived by faith, trusting the Lord to provide. Father was not pleased with the idea of "this life of faith." To his mind it was plain charity and he could not allow his daughter to depend on this type of life! Enough said.

Within a short period, Father came out with a great idea to

help. Aware of Frank's love of timbers and woodwork, as well as his training as a fine woodworker and cabinet maker, he offered Frank a fully-equipped workshop and a shed full of dry timber ready to start production, and ten years' grace to pay for everything. His scheme would be a help for the young couple to have a better start in their married life. But Frank told him that his call from God was to preach and teach the Gospel as a missionary, not to be employed in making money.

It was a similar temptation as the one offered by Frank's former boss in Scotland when he called Frank aside and offered him a partnership in his company, which would have meant a big step up on the ladder of success for Frank.

*(Several years later, during his first furlough, Frank went to visit his old boss, and was amazed at the progress they had experienced with the partner who took Frank's place. In spite of all that, Frank would not have traded what he had with the Lord for anything. "Not for all the tea in China" was his favourite expression!)*

About the same time, Frank had a bad experience. He had borrowed a camera and knowing it was an expensive one he placed it in a small case to keep it out of sight and temptation. But, lo and behold, it was snatched from his hand by a thief. His reaction was to the fact that "It was borrowed". He did not have the money to replace it. What should he do? He decided to try to find temporary work with some American oil companies and went for some interviews. He found suitable work, but before he was engaged, he was told he would have to change his "missionary status" in his passport to be able to take up the position in the company. Once again Frank was faced with the temptation to enter into a money-making situation - he who had bound himself by faith to serve the Lord without looking at 'filthy lucre'!

Shortly after that experience, Frank received a letter from Sam Lander, a Scottish missionary, who had just returned from a furlough. While on furlough he had visited some assemblies in North America. One of these, an assembly from Sault Ste. Marie, had asked him to name a project so that the Ladies Group could work together to help. Sam wrote them back saying: "Nothing for the Landers, but there is a young couple who will be marrying soon."

*Frank & Blanquita*

The Ladies Missionary Group worked and prepared things for a "Wedding shower". It must have been a proper busy time for them, because the things they put in the trunk for the "unknown couple" were astonishing. Everything new, well planned to start a home, plus a few items of clothing for Frank. They added a book, "Plant of Renown" by L. Sheldrake, which was enjoyed and lovingly kept.

The trunk arrived for Frank in Santa Cruz. He brought it to my home to show us the lovely gifts. My parents were "oohing" and "aaahing" all the time. So was I, of course. But the outstanding word came out of my father's lips when he said, "Wonderful. Now, all you need is the furniture!" With this, he pronounced his blessing on the coming marriage, realizing that he could entrust his daughter to that life she was to share with the "unemployed" missionary.

We fixed our wedding date for March 1953 in Santa Cruz. Ned was to be the Best Man! Who else? Frank had promised his elders in Glasgow that he would not get married until he had been two full years in Bolivia.

For the wedding, Frank had instructed me to arrive two or three minutes late, to keep people in suspense and show I had the usual bridal nerves. But when I arrived, I was taken into a side room and had to wait almost 30 minutes! The tailor was desperately trying to finish sewing Frank's jacket. Finally, practical Ned suggested that he give Frank his jacket, and he would take a loan of somebody else's to allow the waiting couple to go through the wedding ceremony. How thoughtful of him!

We went off to honeymoon in a ranch. Part of wedded bliss was horse riding with the cowboys, mustering cattle into the corrals. Frank and I loved horse riding! We were also getting ready for our transition to a new life in Portachuelo, a town to the north of Santa Cruz.

Prior to the wedding we had been planning to settle down to

work in a small town to the north of Santa Cruz. Frank had visited all that area and we felt we could serve the Lord in those places, where both of us had open doors. We felt that Portachuelo would be appropriate since Frank had made many contacts during his travels. But we could not find a house to rent, no timber to make furniture, nothing. The doors were hermetically sealed. Why?

*Chapter 21*

# OFF TO VILLAZON

One day during our honeymoon at the ranch, a cable arrived inviting us to come to Villazon, a town on the border with Argentina, to allow Ron and Mavis Randall to go home on furlough to New Zealand. Right away we realized the reason for the closed doors to Portachuelo. The Lord was moving us to a different part of the country.

Ronald and Mavis Randall were brother and sister to Albert and Eileen Randall, two couples commended as missionaries from New Zealand. Eileen and Albert made their home in Tupiza as well as travelling to the surrounding areas. Tupiza is a small city, situated on the railway line four hours before reaching Villazon at the Argentinian border. When we were living in Villazon we were able to visit Bert and Eileen from time to time as Frank and Bert went on missionary trips to different areas in the vast Andean plateau. Tupiza is at a lower altitude than Villazon and is situated in a valley whose climate allows trees to grow and it boasts some gardens, an attractive relief for people who grew up in the lowlands.

Villazon is on the Andean plateau at an altitude of 12,000 feet above sea level. The climate is cold the year round although the sunshine everyday makes life bearable. Being a town on the Argentinian border and sitting on the railway line linking Bolivia to Argentina, it mainly survives because it is a centre of goods crossing the border. It was a big change for us both moving there. For me, it was a completely new country: cold, no trees, no rain, and a different type of people, who spoke little Spanish as the Quechua language was used by almost all the residents. It was totally different from the low lying tropical Western side of Bolivia!

Soon after our arrival we were able to attend the wedding of Ned and Flora in June 1953 in Tupiza under the hospitality of Bert and Eileen Randall. The wedding was a time of much joy and happiness, with several missionary friends who had travelled to Tupiza to participate in the happy event.

*(After the wedding, Ned and Flora moved to Villamontes, in the hot lowland area of the Bolivian Chaco. A great work was carried on in the town and surrounding area. People heard the message of the Gospel of grace and many were saved and so the work was established. Ned and Flora were very active in contacting people. Flora used her nursing skills to help those who needed to learn more about family guidance, hygiene, etc. Her midwifery training was also very useful in helping women in the town. They soon saw people responding to the message of the Gospel and an assembly was started in Villamontes, the first in the Bolivian Chaco.*

*Ned also started to work with honey bees, something he had done in Australia. He taught some men who were interested to learn the skill as a new trade to help their income. People were very poor but as they were converted to the Gospel they started learning new ways to improve their way of life where all they had known before was to waste their wherewithal in vice and drink. Homes were changed when the Lord came into their lives. The marvel of it all was that the new believers were keen to share the blessing with family and friends, and later went to visit the surrounding little towns and villages with the message of Salvation.)*

In the town of Villazon, Frank and I carried on the work begun by Ron and Mavis, and also crossed the border to La Quiaca, a town where there was a small group of believers on the Argentinian side. The Lord blessed the work in both places. It was there that I, Blanquita, learned a lesson never to be forgotten.

One night a woman in La Quiaca approached me expressing her desire to know more about salvation. It was quite late and it was cold. We still had to walk back across the border to our home in the Bolivian side. I told her I would visit her home the next day. Selfishly, I wanted to go home to warm up a little.

I dutifully went to see her the next day to find her in bed exhausted. Her return home the night before had been nightmarish. She had had to lean on her young daughter most of the way home, resting from time to time with the horrible pain of the cancer from which she was suffering. Her prayer had been, "Lord, keep me alive till tomorrow, until she tells me the way and the truth". She made it home, but was very ill all night and into the next day. As we spoke together, she could not stop from praising the Lord for giving her time to hear the Word and to be delivered from a lost eternity.

As I listened to her, I realized how selfish I had been. It was like a knife piercing my heart, teaching me the urgency of giving the message at the right time, not when it suited me. I remembered how I had been terrified of death when I was convicted of my need of salvation. She was gloriously saved, and I learned an important lesson to last for the rest of my life.

In Villazon, we also learned the important lesson about God's provision coming at the perfect time. A Saturday arrived. We didn't have much money left. So, we put aside the Lord's portion for the next day, and then looked everywhere for coins that sometimes get forgotten in pockets or dropped behind furniture. With what we found we went to market, and managed to buy a bunch of carrots. We could have rice with carrots for our midday meal that day. "Thank You, Lord!"

Next morning, we were startled by a demanding knock on the door at 6.00 a.m. We quickly opened the door to find a dear believer we had met in Cochabamba who had been very kind to us. She had a little basket of good things, fresh cheese, nice Tupiza bread, oranges and other things which we would never have bought ourselves. We were abundantly supplied without having any money. Our Father in Heaven knows our needs!

But He can also use the unexpected.

In the assembly, there was a woman called Felicidad ("Happiness"). She seemed anything but happy, always grumbling and always a sour look on her face. Nothing could make her smile. She was a believer and her husband was an elder in the little assembly. But Felicidad seemed miserable and miserly, desperately clinging to her belongings.

One day, Frank suggested that the elders' meeting be held in our house where it would be warmer than the hall. (We lived in the Randalls' house next to the chapel.) Frank suggested to me it would be nice to prepare a meal for the men. I looked at the almost bare bones of the piece of lamb hanging outside, which functioned as our refrigerator (remember that the temperature at that altitude is almost polar cold). I could produce a stew, but needed potatoes to make the meat go further. There was a knock at the door. Felicidad walked in holding a little round basket of potatoes for me! I said, "Sorry, I can't buy them. I have no money." She said and gestured, "For you ... For you ... no money ... gift ..." The men ate their plentiful stew, thanks to Felicidad.

A wonderful lesson given through a little basket of potatoes. God uses different people and methods to send the needed supply.

Soon it was time to receive Ron and Mavis back from their furlough. During our stay in Villazon, we were blessed by the arrival of our son Ian in 1954. The question again arose, "Where to, Lord?" Soon there was another invitation to replace a missionary couple during their furlough. This time it was Dr. and Mrs. Brown, who lived in Alkatuyo, Potosí among Quechua people.

## Chapter 22

# OUR TURN IN ALKATUYO

I had heard about Alkatuyo and the work of Dr. and Mrs. Brown from Ned and Flora (introduced in Chapter 15), but it was another thing to encounter it in real life! Alkatuyo was at an even higher altitude than Villazon on the arid Andean Plateau and, without a town infrastructure, there was no place to buy foodstuffs. Once a month we had to go to the city of Potosi to get the post, buy supplies, and get the general goods for the month. During our time in Alkatuyo if meat was needed, it had to be bought on the hoof. Live chickens and live sheep. We could buy canned meats in Potosi, but that was too costly.

The missionary work in that area consisted mainly of going to different market fairs around the areas. These were bartering markets, where people brought what they had to trade for whatever they wanted to acquire. I recall having to swallow my disappointment when I couldn't buy some needed fruit and potatoes because all I had was money; no sugar, salt, or any other goods to trade for what we needed. Even our sweaters or shoes would have been accepted! Anything other than money. Cash was worthless in those markets.

Cooking was another trial for a lowlander. Since the boiling point of water is at a much lower temperature at high altitude, everything took 3-4 times longer to get soft and edible. One day, Frank came home proudly bringing a new acquisition: a large pressure cooker he had bought from missionaries moving to lower altitudes. The pressure cooker was a staple piece of equipment by missionaries or foreigners working in the Altiplano. It shortened the cooking time. This precious piece of equipment became my best friend and earned its preferential place in the kitchen! (*I was so fond of the old pressure cooker that it was a staple of my kitchen thereafter, even at sea level, and something I enjoyed cooking in.*)

In Alkatuyo there was a very faithful Quechua believer named Juan de la Cruz Mamani (usually called Juandela). He was a "cacique" (chieftain) among the Quechua people in the area, a social rank reaching back to the Inca Empire. The chieftain of an area and his family were expected to keep a vigilant eye on the community and had communal authority to act as police if need be.

Juandela was such a cacique. He walked and talked like a chieftain, erect and tall, displaying authority. But when he was reached by the Lord, he found the Ultimate Authority and it made a big difference. Being a cacique, his conversion added strength to the preaching of the Gospel in the area. He was ready to help and give witness to what the Gospel had done in his life.

His son Pablo was also very active in the work. He was a great help to Frank with his knowledge of the culture and geography, and he accompanied Frank to the villages and country areas where market fairs took place. Both men got up at the crack of dawn and went to the fair, arriving while the people were still setting up their wares. They preached the Gospel and gave out tracts to all and sundry, until approximately midday when drinking of chicha began and people could become quite aggressive when drunk - with one another and definitely against outsiders. Things could turn ugly in an instant.

One day Frank and Pablo Mamani went to the fair at San Lucas. There was a good reception to the Gospel tracts and to the preaching, so Frank grew enthusiastic seeing the interest of the people and continued preaching past the safe time of day. Suddenly, Pablo grabbed him by the arm and dragged him to the truck, telling him, "Hermano (brother), start the truck urgently." Frank was surprised, but obeyed the instructions. Pablo jumped on to the truck bed, and started trying to calm the incensed people who were shouting angrily and pelting them with stones. Their lives were saved thanks to the quick reaction of dear brother Pablo.

*(Pablo Mamani became a wonderful servant of God. He moved among the immigrant settlers opening new ground in Santa Cruz. He moved to different areas, working the land, but also faithfully preaching the Gospel. He would visit our home in the city of Santa Cruz to get Scriptures, tracts, booklets to give around to the people he reached. Later he learned to use films and videos for evangelistic outreach. I fondly remember his visits, listening to his stories of reaching out to people wherever he was living. He always kept his bearing and posture as a Quechua cacique, but he never pushed himself as someone special. When there was a conference or some other type of gathering, he was always present as a humble servant of the Lord of all.)*

About 25 Km. away from Alkatuyo in a village called Puna, a small group of believers gathered on Sundays for the Breaking of Bread at the house of a poor man called Cirilo Avendaño.

Cirilo had been one of the first believers in the area to come to the Lord and was very faithful. Despite being poor (like many older Quechua beyond their productive years) he also was a high-ranking Quechua, and keeper of the "Khipu", a record-keeping system for the crop rotations and obligatory service in the community. (The Khipu is a system devised of knots tied in a series of strings, themselves tied to a central cord. The decimal-based Inca system of knots was used for both accounting and recording historical events and was so complex that the required training would today be considered like a university education.)

His grown-up sons professed faith as well, but some had moved away. He also had a young daughter by a second wife, who had died when the child was around 4 years old. I don't even remember being aware of the child at the time, but many years later she entered our lives in an interesting way.

*(In the late 1970s, a woman approached me on behalf of her aunt Maria, a Quechua woman from Potosi, who was looking for work as a maid in a Christian home. I tried to find a place for her but no one wanted her, and since I was also needing home help I engaged her to live and work in our home. One could sense she had experienced a lot of suffering. She seemed to live in fear of everything and would rarely dare open her mouth to speak even about daily events, and even then she was barely audible. There were times when I felt she should go.*

*One day I asked her, "Where do you come from, Maria?" She said, "From Puna, Potosí." I then said, "I know Puna. We used to go for Sunday meetings and we met in the house of a man called Cirilo Avendaño".*

*"That was my father", she said. Unlike me, she did remember me*

*from our time in Puna, and she used to dream that it would be marvellous to work for the lovely missionary family!*

*From that day she began to change. Little by little she began to open her heart about the suffering and poverty she had lived under, made worse after her father died. Her half-brothers sent her to work in the fields as an unpaid peon. Eventually, she had managed to leave the village and move to the city where she worked as an unpaid maid servant for one of her half-brothers. She eventually escaped from the slavery her brothers had kept her in, working at whatever she could find, learning the hard way and moving toward the lowlands to work in the sugar cane fields and in the cotton harvest.*

*As Maria stayed in our home, she found love and a family atmosphere. She was able to grow out of her fears. She adopted us as family and became a member of our family for over 30 years! She came to us as a person who never had any schooling, but learned to read and write. She studied Emmaus courses and also learned how to use a computer to enable her to communicate with us by email when we were away from Santa Cruz.*

*She was a great help to me at home and also in the assembly. As a willing helper and servant among God's people, her desire was to be able to look after us till the Lord called us to His presence. Although she was my faithful help in nursing Frank through his final days, she developed stomach cancer, which cut her life short at the age of 58 years. I nursed her as she was called to His presence.*

*As we deal with people and seek to lead them to faith in the Lord, often they come with a heavy baggage of broken lives and suffering. It takes time to help them into new life in Christ.)*

During our time in Alkatuyo, Frank decided to have a

conference for all the believers to take place in the grounds of Dr. Brown's house. Seventeen adults came for the conference from different places. It was a nice time to be together enjoying fellowship around the Word for a full day.

*(About 15 years later we returned for a visit to the area. There was a conference taking place and we managed to arrive just in time for it. It took place on the flat top of a hill, in the open air. You may wonder why. Quite simply, there was no building big enough to hold all the people who came!*

*Outside under the burning sun of the altiplano, the men took off their hats and held them above their faces to protect themselves from the hot sun. Their sense of respect for the Lord would not allow them to have their heads covered. The women were happy to keep their hats on!*

*These conferences were where Frank blossomed as a gifted teacher of the Word. Such was the hunger for God's Word, that conferences of elders from outlying communities could last 3 days, with 14 hours of teaching per day starting in the early morning until late at night. The strength of the Quechua oral culture was such that the elders could transmit almost exactly what they heard to their own assemblies. Frank felt a terrible weight of responsibility in preaching, as elders would quote his exact words from previous conferences when asking questions!)*

During the time in Alkatuyo, our second son, Liam, was added to the family. Around the time he was born (May 1955), we received an urgent request for help from Mr. & Mrs. Gordon Turner, New Zealand missionaries, working in the city of Sucre. Mr. Turner had a health problem and needed to go to Chile for medical care but help was needed in the assembly and to help look after their children,

We moved to Sucre with our two babies and stayed with the Turner family. The health emergency and trip to Chile also provided a needed rest for the parents. We learned they had been back only once to New Zealand with their young children. It is easy to understand. A missionary gets so caught up with the work in the foreign field that it is a hard break to leave on furlough. When you see lives reached with the Gospel and lives transformed, going back to the home country is quite a wrench. The new believers become like your own children. We see how the apostles expressed that feeling in the Epistles.

After that period in Sucre, we returned to the Alkatuyo area till Dr. and Mrs. Brown returned from their furlough.

One day a man came to the Browns' home from the regional school in Alkatuyo, which served as a link for all civil services. A cable from Scotland had arrived at the school for the missionary Haggerty. It brought the sad news that Frank's Dad, William, had passed away from a heart attack in his home. It was a sad time for us both. For Frank, because he would not see his beloved Dad this side of Heaven, a sadness that was tempered by the knowledge that he now was in the Lord's Presence. For me, because I had been looking forward to meet the man who had the difficult task of bringing up three young boys, unaided, and during one of the worst times felt in the last century, the Great Depression.

## Chapter 23

# WHERE TO NOW?

Packing time, readying the house to welcome Roger and Adell Brown back to Alkatuyo, it was time to start looking to the Lord for our new sphere of service. The daily prayer was, "Where can we serve You, Lord?" There were four or five possible places but, "Where do You want us to go, Lord?"

We finally felt the place to go was to the small town of Uyuni, important because it is situated near the well-known Salar de Uyuni, the largest Salt Lake in the world. It is also important because the railway workshop was in Uyuni, making it a transport hub. Four rail lines join here, La Paz, Potosí, Chile, and Villazon on the Argentinian border, making the place an important junction between Argentina, Chile and Peru.

The railway was a lifeline in the Altiplano. It was also a way of life for the merchants who travelled buying and selling supplies from the different areas. Early memories of life in the Altiplano is listening for the bell announcing the arrival of the train, people running to see what the merchants were offering from the windows, be it fruits or whatever else they were taking to sell. Unfortunately in Uyuni trains always arrived between 2 and 6 am. Not a very encouraging time to leave a warm bed, unless there was a dire need!

Uyuni was also a link to small surrounding villages and to many mining towns. The Gospel had been well received, but at the same time the enemy had sown a terrible division. So much so, that a few years earlier, when Frank accompanied Bert Randall, N.Z., on a missionary trip to Uyuni, they were not welcomed at all. In fact, some people called them "Christian Lepers". They returned home broken-hearted. Such a wonderful area. So many opportunities but why was it so difficult to gain entry? But that was where we were off to.

(*Several years later reading the 1995 book "La Gran Conquista" (The Great Conquest) by Eliseo Zúñiga, who details the beginning of the missionary work in Bolivia, I was really amazed to learn of the many missionaries who had laboured in Uyuni, at different times, both as single ladies and couples. What had caused people to become so bitter against missionaries?*)

The Browns were happy to be back and it was time for us to make our way to Uyuni via the city of Potosí. Baby Liam had been unwell so we hoped Dr. Percy Hamilton (Dr. George Hamilton's son) would be in town to give us advice. Unfortunately, he and his wife were away on a missionary trip, so we took Liam to another doctor. He said: "dehydration". Nothing much. "Give him this, give him that."

Since the doctor did not seem to think there was anything serious, we made arrangements to continue on to Uyuni on the next train going out that evening, which would arrive in Uyuni early next morning. The railway line links Potosí to the main line in Uyuni and passes through the highest commercial railway pass in the world called "Paso del Condor," (Condor's Pass) referring to the Condor which is the massive high-flying vulture of the

Andes. There are only two classes on the train. We went into first class. Second class is impossible. Everybody packs in, sitting, standing, bags and boxes all over, plus a good variety of odours, smells and sights. Human sardines without oil, only odours!

After midnight, our little Liam took a turn for the worse. He had been vomiting what little he took in, then became listless. Now he was less and less responsive. As desperate parents we prayed over him, certain we would lose him before the train arrived at a town where we could find help. Frank went to see if he could find a doctor travelling on the train. No one in first class. He went into second class, looking for whatever help he could find. Nothing. It was a time when you have to look up because there was nothing to help at human level.

Then a Quecha chiftain (known by his garb) and considerably taller than most indigenous people came and gave him some coca leaves. He told Frank to put the leaves into the baby bottle and to go and ask for hot water in the kitchen to put in the baby bottle. "Feed this to the baby." We did everything as told, and prayed, each of us in an agony of silent prayer. By this time the baby was cold, with what seemed the sweat of death on his forehead. More silent desperate prayer. Between 2 and 3 a.m. I looked again. Liam was sleeping, warm and pink faced. Normal. "Frank, look at Liam." Frank was afraid to look, but he did so and could scarce believe his eyes. Our Liam was back to full health and never looked back from that time onward. He was our miracle baby!

Frank said, "I have to look for the Indian man". He went back into the second class coaches and asked if anyone had seen the man. Despite the man being so tall, distinctive and distinguished, no one had seen him. There was no one to thank, except the Lord.

Over time and given the circumstances, Frank came to the conclusion that we had experienced angelic ministry. Everything about the man was remarkable from the way he looked, to the fact that he approached Frank. Usually Quechua don't speak to whites unless spoken to, nor is it usual to share their precious coca leaf. It was a preparation for the spiritual warfare that was awaiting us in Uyuni.

# Chapter 24

# UYUNI

We arrived in the early morning. Freezing weather. Praising the Lord for our baby being back to his healthy self, we settled down to acquaint ourselves with our new sphere of service. We took a room in a hotel until we could contact some faithful believers. We were glad to see our boys taking well to the new environment, provided they were properly dressed for the cold.

Uyuni is always cold. It was summer when we arrived and so maybe less cold, but still icy. Most of the year the temperature falls below zero degrees in the evening. In the daytime, temperatures never rise above the low twenties at noon time. There is no rain during the months of March to October/November. During the summer months rain usually falls as snow or hail.

Uyuni was founded toward the end of the 18th Century. Later the railway lines were built by British engineers to facilitate the transport of minerals on their way to ports on the Pacific Ocean. It became a key town on the railway line which linked Bolivia with Argentina and Chile. Set at an altitude of 12,000 feet above sea level in the middle of the vast open expanse of the great Andean plateau and the flat salt lake, there is nothing to stop the North to South winds that bring bitter cold. When the wind arrived in the town, it was channelled by the houses and became stronger, combining with particles of sand and hitting the bare legs of the women and children like sandpaper.

The cold was formidable. We were told many horror stories of people caught outdoors overnight who were found frozen solid the next day. The year before we came to Uyuni, a military group had a problem with their vehicle in the Salt Lake. In desperation they burned everything that could be burned in order to fight the intense cold. The entire group were found dead the next day. Unlike now, in those days there were no mobile communication systems.

(*In 2011, a family on a sightseeing trip got lost in the sea of salt with their vehicle. They were going round in circles but could not find their way out. The problem in that vast expanse of white salt is the lack of landmarks to guide one. The family was saved thanks to a cellular phone. The wonders of modern technology!*

*The Salt Lake is a solid flat plain of salt. When the rains come in the summer, the water accumulates on the surface and the lake becomes a disorienting mirror until evaporation takes place. When it dries, any land marks erected before have been washed out during the rainy season.*

*During all the years we lived in Uyuni, I never set foot on the Sea of Salt. Sometimes travelling I would see the white glistening expanse of the salt disappearing into the horizon, that was all. I had to smile when, looking in the Internet for details about salt, I found a lot of information about Uyuni, the place where we had lived for several years. Only then I was able to 'visit' the famous Salt Lake of Uyuni and study all its wonders. Small consolation in my old age!*)

Frank went around contacting some of the believers he had

met on earlier visits. Over the years, several missionaries had visited and resided in Uyuni for periods of times, always seeking to sow the seed of the Gospel. Undoubtedly, their time spent in Uyuni left a deep impression. Blessing was seen among the people. But there is always an Enemy and problems appeared that spoiled the work.

One problem arose from Exclusive teaching that caused terrible division among the believers. Its effects were crystalized in the attitude toward missionaries. The Exclusive group was aggressive against the missionary brethren, treating them as lepers and outcasts, even if they had been close friends before. But there were the few who remained loyal to the ones who brought the message to them.

Frank contacted faithful friends like Lucio and Alicia Ramirez, who made us very welcome. The Ramirezes had opened their home to have the church meetings for the few who wanted to remain together. The Exclusive group tried to take benches and other things that belonged to the assembly, but the few faithful kept the things under lock and key, praying that someone would come to help, so when Frank visited them, he was made very welcome. We had an open door to the work in Uyuni among this group.

After a few days in the hotel, we had a visit by Crispin Huanca. He offered us a room in his house till we could find a place to rent. We were thankful for the offer. We moved there where we had half the space of a store room. Crispin's mother was very hostile to the missionaries and did everything possible to show her dislike. In spite of her attitude to us, some years later the Holy Spirit touched her heart and she was gloriously saved and her attitude totally changed.

Many years before, Crispin had played an interesting role in famous incident. In the late 1940s, an Uyuni man who owned a "miraculous Virgin Mary" statue believed the Gospel message, started reading his Bible and became troubled in his soul about idol worship. The man felt he could not give away the statue to anyone, so he decided to destroy it. He asked the missionary, John Munro Perry (N.Z.), to drive him to a place far out of the town, where he proceeded to break his statue down into powder to avoid further idolatry.

*Frank at Uyuni*

When the townspeople became aware of what had happened, they were furious and angry, not against the owner but against the "Protestants". A mob gathered to go to the Perry house with the clear intention of hanging him in the Plaza. But before they arrived, someone came with the news that he had seen the missionary's jeep going toward Pulacayo (a nearby mining town). Realising the futility of hanging someone who was not there, the mob dispersed. In fact, it was not Mr. Perry but Crispin Huanca who was driving the jeep, having borrowed it to help in the meeting at Pulacayo. Since trusting the Lord a few years earlier, Crispin was a great helper to the work. Unknown to the mob, God was in control, protecting His servants.

(In fact a few days later, soldiers came to the missionaries' house and escorted Mr. Perry and his family away from danger of mob violence. They took him to La Paz where he was thrown into the Panóptico, a famous prison, to await sentence. The British Consul intervened and eventually managed to get the family free on condition of being deported from the country. Both husband and wife had to leave Bolivia for a number of years until the anger died down.)

We appreciated having a roof over our heads. Eventually, we found a house to rent and dedicated much time to visit the believers. But there were many lessons to be learned by the newly-arrived housewife!

Water for Uyuni was brought from a distant lake, mainly because the railway engines needed good, soft water to avoid calcium deposits in the boilers (for which I was very thankful!). But as the temperature goes down, pipes freeze and burst and so the water supply is turned off through the night hours. One had to keep water in pails. One lesson to be learned for the morning cup of tea or coffee was to have water already in your kettle, because there would be a couple of inches of ice in the pail of water that had to be broken before the kettle could be filled for breakfast!

If the newly arrived housewife delayed hanging the washing out early then by 4.00 p.m. it would be frozen onto the line. It couldn't be taken down and folded. It was like handling unwieldy pieces of plywood. Then one had the problem of the sheets, and all else defrosting inside the house.

A boon was the fact that things didn't rot. We lived in a permanent refrigerator. Unlike the tropics where things spoil between the morning and evening, here everything froze unless care was taken. This was good for meats and cooked meals, but vegetables had to be covered and insulated since potatoes and other vegetables change their texture and flavour (for the worse!) if they are allowed to freeze and thaw. In the market everything is kept well covered under the roof.

Another new experience was shopping. The "llameros" (llama drovers) brought their produce from the valleys at lower altitude to trade for salt from Uyuni that was extracted from the shores of the lake. During those years, supplies were quite scarce. Meat had to be bought early in the morning, so one had to be out of the warm bed and run to queue up in the market. There were items that couldn't be found in the stores or market. One had to go to the railway station and buy it from the passengers, but that meant running to the Uyuni Station when one heard the trains arrive. The need had to be very real to venture going out into the arctic temperature between midnight and 6 am.

A new sight for us was the few trees that graced the Railway Avenue being covered with hessian cloth during the winter months. They would be uncovered when the weather started warming up!

Fortunately, no cockroaches, mosquitos or the like were found in Uyuni. But woe of woes, in the summer, we were visited by flies. The flies turned the white ceilings into mottled black. Lazy flies hovering over everything made me think they also suffered from high altitude problems, yet they were wily enough to avoid being swatted to death.

It was during that time, 1956, the news came over the radio of the massacre of the five missionaries in Ecuador. We were all shocked and turned to prayer for the widows and children. It set a mark in our lives. These were young missionaries like ourselves, who had poured themselves out for the Lord's Service. Frank took Jim Elliot's words as his own vision: "He is no fool who gives up what he cannot keep to gain what he cannot lose".

(*New Tribes Mission experienced a similar tragedy in the jungles of Santa Cruz in the latter part of 1946 when five missionaries were massacred by the jungle natives. Many new missionaries, men and women, took up the call and worked tirelessly till they reached several fierce tribes with the Gospel. And once again with the massacre in Ecuador the famous Tertullian phrase, "The blood of the martyrs is the seed of the church," was proved to be true. Churches everywhere were awakened to the stark reality that people out there need missionaries to take the Gospel of Christ to them.*)

*Chapter 25*

# WELCOME AT LAST

The believers who had remained faithful welcomed us and helped in every possible way to make our settling down easier. The Exclusive camp showed real hostility, trying to discredit us in every possible way, and attacking those believers who attended our meetings or had any contact with us. Sometimes a contentious man would come in during the meetings and enter into a big confrontation with Frank while the people witnessed their false accusations and innuendo. The same happened when they saw Frank in the street. They would come and start shouting at him. Frank let them have their say, pointed to the Scriptures and tried to bade them a friendly goodbye.

Around Uyuni there were many small towns, villages and settlements. There were also several large mining towns with groups of believers gathering to the Name of the Lord. One of the villages called Chacala became unbelievably transformed through their accepting the Gospel message. People wanting to please the Lord banned drunkenness and debauchery of any kind. Even the yearly celebration of Carnival was banned. It was forbidden to bring alcohol in any shape or form to the village. They were eager to go around witnessing and preaching to other villages.

Crispin Huanca placed himself at Frank's disposal to take him to visit different groups of believers. Many places were visited, even across the Salt Lake. They often went at the invitation of someone who desired to hear more about the Bible. After several visits others were saved and they had the joy of seeing a new small assembly gathering to remember the Lord.

In contacts with the people it became known that don Francisco (his Spanish name) was married to a Bolivian woman. Well, the news provoked an incredible reaction. The Quechua mind worked it out in the following way: "The Word teaches that man and wife are one. If don Francisco is married to a Bolivian, then he has become a Bolivian. He is one of us!" It became God's way for Frank to find acceptance in working around the villages among the Quechua and Aymará people, many times bridging the gap that had been established by the division.

While in Uyuni a baby girl arrived, Jeannie, a sister to Ian and Liam. We had great joy in and with our children but we had to be very careful to keep them away from unhealthy places. So, as much as I longed to travel and visit the places, we had decided that mother would stay at home with the little ones. Life in those far-out villages was very harsh. Scarcity of water, food and heat would make life very difficult for children in the adobe huts where people dwelt. Frank spent a lot of time away on travel.

Once when Frank went for an entire week with the people across the Salt Lake, all they had to eat was a confection of ground quinoa which is a very good cereal. They grind the quinoa, roll it into balls and steam it. That was all they had to offer the visitors. Frank survived on nothing more than warm water and those "chalky" balls during the entire week! Meanwhile back in the town of Uyuni and unaware of this food ordeal, I decided to make a delicious quinoa dish for his arrival. I never saw such a look of dismay when I brought out my "super delicious dish" to celebrate his return home. "Take THAT away and give me a piece of bread and a cup of tea. I don't want to see quinoa for a long time!" He then proceeded to tell us his quinoa experience. Maybe that is why quinoa has been absent from my kitchen despite its excellent nutritive qualities.

You see, the Quechua/Aymara people have a keen sense of hospitality. They share with you whatever they have, and whatever they bring to you must be eaten or else an offence is created. This can give place to a root of bitterness in relations to one another.

(*About 12 years later, when visiting many places in the Altiplano with our Camper truck and with our teenage children, we arrived at a village where a large conference was being held. In the morning, Frank went in to be with the believers. The children and I stayed in the camper and had breakfast. Shortly after finishing, there was a knock on the door and we found a believer outside inviting all of us to have breakfast in the house. We all set to eating breakfast, again. It consisted of a thick red soup that we discovered was "red hot". It was "coloured" with red chillies! Knowing the family rules that no food could be refused, the children struggled through the spoonfuls until the bowls were clean. That was not the end of it. Our hosts came back offering and insisting on a refill. And then another! At least that was an improvement on when the children were younger and, to avoid offence, the parents had to gulp down the food the children could not finish!*)

Our early years in Uyuni were very lean financially. Gifts from Scotland were slow coming in and not easy to exchange locally. We had to be very creative in finding ways to make ends meet.

But our faith in God's provision was strengthened by the faith and generosity of our fellow believers.

Doña Dominga, an old Quechua widow, was one of the first believers who welcomed us whole-heartedly in Uyuni. One day doña Dominga appeared at our house and handed Frank a wad of cash saying, "Don Francisco, this is my contribution toward our new seats. This is all I have." Frank protested, "No ... doña Dominga, you are a poor widow. You need your savings for everyday expenses!" Dominga wouldn't accept a "No". She rebuked Frank saying, "My God has supplied me all these years of my widowhood and will supply me until I die." Frank was humbled by her attitude, and accepted the offering.

He never forgot doña Dominga's step of faith in God. Her example helped many folks! During the years we lived in Uyuni, the entire community provided for doña Dominga. There was always a plate of food for Dominga, at our table and at many others. Someone would give her a can of milk, or bread, tea, coffee to take home. She was always clean and neat. Her skirts were washed and mended. Out in the country, believers planted a row of potatoes here and there earmarked for Sister Dominga. When the time came for gathering the crops she would travel and get "her row of potatoes" or something else. She was a special person who never outstayed her welcome in any home.

(*Willie and Ray Hill, the Scottish missionaries who came to continue the care of the work in the area, built their own house and included a little room especially for doña Dominga who moved there and was looked after until she went to be with the Lord. What a display of faith by an old Quechua woman who took the Lord at His word and trusted Him to supply all her needs.*)

Another story of exemplary giving was when one of the sisters in the assembly named Julietta decided to take the example of the widow of 1 Kings 17:10-16 and apply it to herself. Looking to the Lord, she started giving a share of their monthly provision of food supplies from the Railway Food Market for railway employees. The provision was carefully meted out according to the number of family members. Julietta and her husband Waldo were faithful believers and assisted us as much as possible when we first arrived in Uyuni.

One afternoon I saw Julietta come in to our patio with a can of powdered milk and something else. I thought she was selling the goods. I asked the price and she replied: "It is a gift for you!" Then she told me of how, after listening to the story of the widow of Zarephath, she took the decision to share the provision from the railway with the people the Lord brought to her heart. To her amazement she discovered that food stuffs like rice and sugar which before were only enough for the month, now proved always more than enough.

Eventually Waldo and Julietta moved to Cochabamba after Waldo retired from the railway. Both were a blessing in the development of the assembly work in Cochabamba, and became much appreciated as were their daughters. We learned from Julietta's decision to trust the Lord with the provision of food. God not only supplies but truly showers blessings to the individual and to others around.

The work in Uyuni had grown. Home visitation had been a good tool to break down the distrust toward missionaries. People slowly started to show friendship. The assembly was in a healthy state. The sincere people, who had been scattered through the divisive work, were restored and gathered together again. We were happy. We had become accustomed to the harsh climate. The assembly was in a healthy state and thoughts of building their own meeting place were voiced. Everybody was keen.

We decided it was a good time for furlough. We invited Willie and Ray Hill to relieve us during furlough. And so off we went to Scotland.

*Time in Scotland*

This involved a four-day train journey from Uyuni to Buenos Aires, followed by 28 days aboard the ship to London, then a night train to Glasgow where we were received by a good number of Frank's friends who were keen to receive their missionary with his acquired Bolivian wife and children. I sometimes wonder what kind of person they were expecting. People in the assemblies had formed their image of what they expected. I looked very different. Some girls later voiced their surprise. "You are like us!", they said, "apart from the English language".

Frank was in big demand to give reports about the work in Bolivia. He travelled all over the British Isles. Many people listened to him and much prayer was raised for the Lord's work.

While Frank was travelling, I kept the home fires going, since the small children needed their Mum near. During this furlough our youngest child, Philip, arrived. A little Scottie to join his Scottish Dad! Occasionally I could go to nearby places in the city of Glasgow. Furlough was a learning period for the Bolivian wife, but we all experienced much love and kindness. It shows the wonderful blessing of being in the family of God. "Being in Christ" breaks all barriers.

Then it was time to return to Bolivia. Back to Uyuni.

We discovered that Willie and Ray Hill had also fallen in love with the work there. However they moved to another area of work, because we were returning to continue in the place.

## Chapter 26

# WHERE NEXT?

We were glad to be back. There was so much going on in and around Uyuni.

During our furlough we had obtained camping equipment and supplies to make the travelling to outlying areas safer and more comfortable. Frank kept on the go, visiting many places within travelling distance, always teaching the different groups of believers. Sometimes we went together as a family when we visited small mining towns in the huge area that was open for visits. Frank managed to build a small caravan to be pulled by the truck. It was fitted out for long trips.

Home visitation was a good tool to break down the distrust toward missionaries. People slowly started to show friendship. Sunday school work started. Parents also started attending meetings and enjoying being back to worship in the meeting place. When you have more people you need more seating accommodation. Frank started to worry about needing more benches. The believers were informed of the need to buy timber for the seats. Frank had set up a workshop and offered to do the carpentry work himself, but at the pace that money came in.

But after we settled back into Uyuni, we had to face the

difficult issue of our children's education. Our oldest son Ian was becoming of age to enter school. Education is a difficult issue for missionary parents. They have to take into account the places to which the Lord has called them. Some work with nomadic people who are always on the move, others live in small villages where there is little schooling available. Parents also have to make choices that will prepare their children to attend homeland schools during periods of furlough, and in some cases for higher education.

In Bolivia, two missionary groups established schools for missionary children to accommodate these issues. New Tribes Mission, whose missionaries engaged in first contact with unreached peoples, had a boarding school, Tambo, situated around the middle of the 500 Km. road that joins Cochabamba and Santa Cruz. The school offered an American curriculum and was available to other missionaries also.

We made the difficult decision to send little Ian away from Uyuni since the little school in the town was sadly deficient. It was hard to prepare Ian for the separation from his siblings and parents in order to go to a completely new place and be with new people.

The school was about 900 Km. from home in Uyuni. It meant travelling through the flat Altiplano to Oruro, where the road started to descend to the lower altitude of Cochabamba. And what a road that was in those days! I still shudder to remember the many times we had to negotiate huge pot holes, encounter oncoming traffic in narrow areas with me telling Frank not to move another inch, or else the truck would roll over the precipice! We tried to drive all night. In this way we could see the lights of an oncoming vehicle and find a wider spot to await for passing one another. I remember little Ian standing almost all night watching the road. He could not sleep during the trip. He was so different from his brother Liam who went to sleep as soon as the trip started.

So, little Ian was away to school where he had his painful time of adjustment without Dad and Mum. It was also a painful adjustment for his Dad and Mum.

(*We found Tambo to be an excellent school. It offered a high standard in education and a spiritual emphasis. All our children went there and Ian and Liam graduated from High School in Tambo. Missionary kids in years gone by often left the field as young teens and went to the homeland to be cared for by relatives or go to boarding schools. This could be a distressing experience for both parents and children. Some missionary kids could not adjust to life in the "home country", and did not see their parents from one furlough to the next.*

*When the time came to make the decision whether to send Ian to Scotland to have schooling compatible with the British curriculum, we could not bear it. We decided to accept the consequences of giving our children an American rather than a British secondary schooling.*

*During our furlough in Scotland, we had looked into schooling by correspondence. Unfortunately, there was little available and the cost of each course from Britain was beyond our means. The idea of "home schooling", now very popular, was not yet developed.*)

Back in Uyuni life went back to the usual routine. One day a believer from the country came in looking for Frank. I told him to knock on the window where Frank was and continued working in the kitchen across from the bedroom window. Sometime later

I noticed the man was still patiently waiting for Frank (they are very patient). I crossed the patio and looked in at the window, thinking of making a sharp remark on Frank's negligence toward the visitor. To my distress, Frank was stretched out on the floor, unconscious. I asked the believer for help, and between us we lifted him onto the bed. I sent him for the doctor. (There were no phones at the time.) Frank came round and the doctor arrived and examined him. He found nothing other than high blood pressure.

Several months went by. Everything was fine. The end of the year came with the usual activities. Two days before Christmas day, Frank was ill again. The doctor diagnosed "Angina Pectoris" and strongly recommended a lower altitude, because it is a well-known fact that altitude affects lowlanders after some years. We wondered about going to a town, Tupiza, which was about 1500 feet below Uyuni. The doctor said it wasn't low enough to make a difference.

Both of us were heart-broken by the recommendation. Surely we could stay there a bit longer. However, the stress of coping with the dissident believers over several years and the continued activity of travelling around to visit the places where believers were hungry for the teaching of the Scriptures and doing this at high altitude had affected Frank's heart.

Our time in Uyuni had been a blessing to others and to us. We had enjoyed the work. We thought our feet `were firmly planted in the place. We did not think of moving to another place. But God had other plans! We didn't realize that it was God giving us a push. God knew it was time to move. He needed us somewhere else.

Willie and Ray Hill agreed to return to Uyuni. The next few months were spent preparing, searching for an indication of God's will for our future sphere of service. Willie and Ray arrived in Uyuni around the middle of 1961, and entered immediately into the various activities in the work of the Lord. We stored some of our belongings with them, got the caravan ready with the necessary things for the road and off we went.

The time had come to leave Uyuni. But to where?

We had no indication of where we should go. Frank always had a desire to return to the lowlands, which also fitted with the doctor's advice. A couple of years before we had tried to leave the altitude, but had discovered it wasn't God's time. It felt we were like Abraham who went out "not knowing whither he went". We stopped at places on the route visiting believers and staying a week or more as deemed necessary. We stopped in Tupiza, then Villazon where we had spent time at the beginning of our missionary service, then headed toward the South West of Bolivia, slowly descending to lower altitudes.

*Caravan*

Finally, we arrived at Bermejo, a small town on the Southern border with Argentina, where there was a single missionary manning the assembly work. George Martin from Scotland was glad of the visit and the company. (It is good to have a change of voice, in the assembly and in the home!) But Bermejo had a double pest: mosquitos at sundown, and a pesky small gnat with a very itchy bite during daylight! Our youngest boy, Philip, suffered so much from mosquito bites that we thought we needed to leave. The poor child was continually covered with red, itchy sores. He scratched them continually into open sores. He was a painful sight.

George had taken training at the Missionary School of Medicine in London learning a lot about Homeopathic Medicine and offered to help our poor Philip. He studied the case and prepared a dose of medicine which might help or prove a failure. He treated the three-year-old boy to which was added much prayer from all of us. The medication worked and the horrible itching left Philip forever! (*I checked up with Philip in later years about bug bites. He was happy to report that he gets the red welt after the bite, but it soon disappears.*)

After spending several weeks in Bermejo, it was time to move on seeking the place of the Lord's choosing, much to George's disappointment at losing friends and companions so soon. We left, heading this time further west, to Villamontes, a small town which had been right in the middle of things during the Chaco war between Bolivia and Paraguay, where Ned and Flora Meharg had settled after their marriage.

Ned loved the tropical heat there, and he tried to teach the menfolk how to improve the way they worked in order to earn a better income. Flora helped with nursing care. They were accepted and loved by all. Many children born under Flora's nursing care were named after them! Ned and Flora also visited the area around Villamontes, taking the Word to villages, and even contacting the Indigenous Mataco peoples. As they became known, the people started to accept the message of the Gospel, were saved and baptized and a small assembly started.

Ned and Flora gave us a great welcome. They also shared with us their exercise about a new field of work. The assembly was in a condition to be able to continue without missionaries. Ned invited us to stay in their home to allow them to travel to Cobija, Pando, the Northernmost part of Bolivia bordering Brazil, to explore the possibility of a new work there. We accepted the invitation because we knew the Lord would have us continue waiting on Him.

Three months later, Ned and Flora returned with glowing reports about the open door in Cobija. In all their visitation there they had found only one evangelical believer! People were thirsting for the Gospel message. The Mehargs realized the way was open for them. The believers in Villamontes let them go with much sorrow, but realized the Lord was calling them to take the Gospel to other areas in the country.

(*Ned and Flora started a pioneer work for the Lord in the town of Cobija, and the villages in the surrounding country areas. Pando had been a much-neglected part of the country politically, administratively and in every sense.*

*The people mainly lived from gathering Brazil nuts in the forest. Travel was rudimentary, mostly by navigating the rivers during the high water season, though there was a small airport with a couple of flights per week. Supplies were very expensive as most things had to be flown in from other cities.*

*Eventually Ned and Flora also travelled the rivers visiting outlying villages. They met many problems. One day when Ned was fixing his boat on the beach, he stepped on an electric sting ray, receiving a terrible electric shock and the venomous barb implanted in his leg prostrated him for a few weeks and damaged his heart. After many years of service in Cobija, the work was well established, with responsible local workers carrying on with the activities. This allowed the Mehargs to move to a different area where again they were well used.)*

It was also time for us to leave Villamontes. We were heading for Santa Cruz to see my family, hopefully in time for Christmas.

## Chapter 27

# THE LOWLANDS

The trek heading for Santa Cruz was punctuated by amusing events, like buying a watermelon for the road, eating it and finally using the rind to wash the dust from our faces. Or five-year old Jeannie saying: "Let's go home, Daddy", to which Frank replies "Where is home, Jeannie?". Or holding bowls to catch the rain leaking from holes in the truck roof so they wouldn't drip down the driver's back only to have the full bowl spilled down Frank's back when the truck hit a bad bump. "Aaah!!!!" And so it went on.

In our hurry to be home by Christmas, we bypassed the town of Camiri, an important oil town south of Santa Cruz, only to be stopped by a Thump! The bolt linking the caravan to the truck broke. Now what? It was a major problem. Truckers stopped to help. When they realized the type of problem, they said: "Go back to Camiri and seek the help of don Eugenio at the school. He is a good man and will be glad to help."

So, Frank went back to the town we had bypassed and met don Eugenio at the Christian school. We received the help needed at the time and we were very glad to have met Eugene and Lorraine Train, fellow missionaries from the U.S.A. (*It was the beginning of a wonderful friendship for all of us. Gene Train, ("don Eugenio" his Spanish name) and his wife Lorraine opened their hearts and home to us from that time on. A few years later we had the privilege of staying in Camiri while they took a short furlough visiting family and friends in the States.)*

After repairing the needed bolt, we continued our trek to Santa Cruz and in the search of the place God had for us. After six months on the roads, we arrived in Santa Cruz. We were still waiting for definite guidance. The only guiding light so far was the doctor's advice for Frank to get away from the high altitude of the Altiplano. The final word would come from the Lord Himself.

One day Mr. Allan Mcleod Smith, missionary from N.Z., asked Frank to drop in for a visit and consultation. He told Frank that Mrs. Smith had been diagnosed with pernicious anemia, and the doctor had advised Mr. Smith to take her to Cochabamba, to a higher altitude. The tropics was detrimental to his wife's health. But in addition to concern about his dear wife's health, he was concerned about his responsibilities in the assembly. Mr. Smith asked Frank if he, we, could come and take up the work they had been engaged in. We gladly accepted the invitation, knowing that God had brought us back at His perfect time.

So at the beginning of 1962 we settled in Santa Cruz. I was back among the people who had seen me grow up in Sunday School, who had witnessed my growing up in the Lord, witnessed my struggle with the crippling arthritis during my teens, who were witnesses at our wedding and who had seen us depart to the Andes. Now we returned as missionaries living among them. Who would have thought it possible!

Personally, I was afraid. Afraid of the dear older sisters whose lives had been a testimony during my struggles growing up. How should I behave toward them? At the first Women's Meeting, I spoke to them and confessed my fears and also admitted how I loved being back with them. I told them I needed to be helped in the work! Please let's work together in harmony and, please, would they let me know if I was missing the mark? They gave us their welcome, and we were off to a good start.

We made one last trip to Uyuni to collect our belongings before settling down to the work in the lowlands of Santa Cruz.

Two interesting events took place in Uyuni. The railway trip to Uyuni was through the night at sub-zero temperature. We were glad to have the sleeping bags we brought from Scotland and we zipped ourselves in. Frank took his shoes off and placed them under the seat. We were fairly comfortable during the night and arrived in Uyuni at 6 am. When Frank looked for his shoes, they were gone! During the night someone had stolen them, right from under him. That was a major problem. Frank was a tall man, six foot three. Naturally he had a good foundation, he wore size 12 shoes, which were not available in Bolivia. It was a real disaster! The thought of a small Quechua man walking in the streets of Uyuni wearing size 12 shoes made me burst out laughing, though Frank didn't think it funny. The ground was freezing cold and not much fun to walk on without shoes!

We went to Willie and Ray Hill's home, walking, of course, there being no taxis in Uyuni in those days. The shoe problem continued. Impossible to borrow shoes from Willie Hill whose feet were smaller. Finally, Frank found a pair of old army boots he had brought from Scotland. They were dreadful looking, ready for the garbage but were all that could be found among our belongings. He was terribly self-conscious of his ugly boots, but they served him until we returned to Santa Cruz where he had other shoes!

The other interesting event was a total solar eclipse that took place while we were there. In Uyuni the eclipse would be total, and there were a good number of astronomers from different countries to observe the event. It was interesting to watch the sun being covered bit by bit. As the sunlight diminished, the temperature went down. Exactly at 11 am. it went dark as night, the temperature was freezing, and there was just a faint circle of light around the edges of the moon. Then the sun started appearing on the other side and the temperature rose.

That experience made me understand why the Incas worshipped the Sun. Especially high in the Andean mountains, the sun is the fountain of light and warmth, the enabler of sowing and reaping so that there might be food for the people.

*Chapter 28*

# GO TELL IT ON THE MOUNTAINS

From Santa Cruz, we continued our friendship and collaboration with Gene and Lorraine Train from Camiri. They had arrived in 1951, following the invitation by other missionaries to help their children with their schooling. Eventually they had the vision of opening a Christian School in Camiri to reach children and parents with the Gospel. They started with lower grades and built up to High School. The school became well known and highly regarded. As time went on, it was quite an honour to have been a student of Camiri Christian School.

During the school holidays, Gene and Lorraine always travelled to the mountains. Camiri is near the foot of the sierras that begin the Andes mountains. Numerous settlers had moved to live and work in the mountains and valleys, where they enjoyed peace from political unrest and found virgin lands which could be worked for agriculture and cattle raising.

The Trains traversed the sierras on horseback visiting farms, villages, and groups of settlers, always seeking to spread the message of Salvation. Opposition was found in most places, because people had been used to the traditional faith throughout their lives. However, the Gospel message touched hearts here and there. People realized this teaching gave them peace in their hearts and what is more the power to overcome sinful customs and habits which often created havoc in their families and social groups.

One man Gene met was Secundino Salinas, an educated man and a small land owner in the area called Huacareta to whom he gave a New Testament to read. Secundino received the New Testament and occasionally he read it.

At that time there was political unrest. There were pro-government groups who would invade properties and take ownership of things, forcibly instituting their version of the land reform. One such group came to Huacareta and rounded up several land owners. There was resistance and several invaders lost their lives. The remaining invaders went back to La Paz and returned with a bigger force and took as prisoners those who had opposed them. They told them to dig graves for themselves. They were to be killed in revenge for what had happened with the previous group. As the land owners were kneeling down by the open graves waiting for the bullets to hit them, a priest came onto the scene. He told the executioners to stop and allow him to pray for the souls of those about to die. They agreed. The priest prayed and prayed and prayed. Finally, the invaders dropped their heavy rifles and announced they would take the prisoners to La Paz instead.

Secundino's head had been whirling with the idea of death. How am I going to present myself before God? Portions of the New Testament came into his mind: "Believe in the Lord Jesus and you shall be saved ..." and other verses also. He believed the Word and knew he was saved. Then he started to pray for his wife that she might find the way too so they could be together in God's presence. That was when he heard they would be taken to La Paz.

When they arrived in the city, they were thrown into a cell. Secundino told his companions of the transaction that had taken place within his soul, and how he had trusted the Lord Jesus as Saviour. His brother-in-law, Jose Saracho, and his nephew, Ovidio, also made a decision for the Saviour that night. Eventually they were allowed to return home. The three men, truly believers in the Lord as Saviour, started to preach the Gospel. Secudino became a caring employer and his life gave testimony to the power of the Gospel.

(*This story is a reminder that God continues working for our salvation even when all hope seems lost.*

*Little by little small groups of believers gathered in the mountain areas. The new Christian parents desired better schooling for their children. Gene and Lorraine received a number of students into their home. These went to school every day, but also helped in the home with chores. A very practical way of training them.*

*Eventually, this led to the creation of a boarding home to house children from the mountain areas.*)

Frank also joined Gene Train in trips to the mountains during school vacations. It was a great return to the adventure of his early missionary days as a Glaswegian Cowboy! They went out on horseback, travelling all day through often dangerous mountain passes. If they came to a farm in a glen, they would stop to visit. Usually the land owner would be glad to break the solitary monotony of mountain life and invite them to stay for a meal and a visit. The group of travellers, usually made up of 5-8 persons, always enjoyed the break and the opportunity to speak about the Lord Jesus and His offer of Salvation.

They did have many harrowing experiences during the trips. A frightening experience was when the horses had to go across a very narrow pass and had to be unloaded. Food, clothes, books had to be carried by hand and reloaded after the horse had safely made it through the pass. One day, following the same pass, Frank's horse lost its footing and fell down taking Frank, his rider, with him. Frank just managed to jump off the horse onto a clear area below and was rescued. His horse disappeared for ever.

Every year they tried to travel further into the canyons, always looking for new territories in the sierras. On one memorable day they arrived in a village which had a Roman Catholic church in the plaza. The people gathered about the visitors wanting to know the reason for the visit. Our friends were grateful for the opportunity and quickly started to preach their message while handing out Gospel literature. However, after a while the priest came out of the church wielding a gun and a big whip which he used against the missionaries, and no less kindly on his own parishioners. He threatened that the visitors would taste the bullets in his gun if they didn't clear out of the village immediately! They quickly moved out saying, "He who runs away, lives to see another day!"

Around that time, we had a visitor from Belfast, Denis Gilpin. He had a tremendous interest in all aspects of the missionary work in Bolivia and he also visited the Trains for a short while.

The time came for one of the mountain trips. This would be quite a challenge for Denis, but no young person is going to say "NO" to adventure. And so he joined the party. A good horse had to be found for the tall Irishman. The group started on their trip. On the second night, his horse ate some "loco" weed, which is very poisonous for horses. In the morning the horses were saddled, loaded, mounted and off they went. Suddenly, Denis's horse shuddered, and collapsed right under him. The horse died instantly and so Denis lost his mount. The party had to rearrange their pack mounts and find a horse for the visitor!

During one of the trips close to Christmas, the travellers were hurrying home to their families. The rainy season was also starting. The group came to a wide river that had to be crossed. Frank was mounted on a horse not used to crossing rivers. It panicked and started taking its head and was getting into deeper and more troubled waters. The others kept shouting and signalling Frank to drive his horse to their side. Unfortunately, the horse was not following directions. The others kept attempting to lasso them but all efforts failed. Frank was heading to certain death.

But one of the younger men who lived in the mountain area, suddenly felt a deep longing to say a last goodbye to the good friends. Quickly he re-saddled his horse and galloped to the side of the river, where he saw brother Frank heading into dangerous waters. He spurred his horse into the raging water, and eventually managed to lasso Frank's horse's head and started inching it back. At the same time, he instructed Frank on how to guide the horse to safety. That is how Frank was saved from drowning!

(*I never heard about the near drowning incident until a couple of years later when I heard the story mentioned during the prayer meeting in Summerfield Hall in Glasgow! Frank later admitted the "omission" had been to spare me pain and worry!)*

Later, as Frank reflected on these events and worked out the time zone difference, he realized that the believers in Summerfield Hall, Glasgow, had been "watching and praying" together in their regular Thursday prayer meeting where they always lifted Frank in prayer. And there in faraway Bolivia, a young man suddenly felt a tremendous desire to go to the river to wave a last goodbye to his missionary friends. He had an experienced river horse, a long lasso, and courage to take action to save one of the Lord's missionary servants. But above all he had the Holy Spirit, with prayer as the added vital ingredient, as it is in all our lives especially those servants of the Lord who daily face attacks from the enemy of our souls. Everybody got home safely. Christmas was enjoyed and life continued as usual.

*(In later years, it was proposed to hold a Conference in Camiri, inviting people from the mountains and nearby towns and villages for a time of teaching and fellowship. It became a tremendous success. People came in droves to the Conference, and many were reached with good teaching of the Scriptures. It started new friendships based on their common faith. Country people contributed foodstuffs and other things toward the feeding of the crowds. Homes were opened to receive visitors wherever they could stretch out their bed rolls.*

*The Conference went on for a number of years reaching attendance of over 1000 people. Everyone looked forward to September. The kitchen area at the Conference was serviced by a great group of solid Christian men and women who had things well organized and enjoyed meeting the needs of visitors and local believers. They served three meals daily to more than 1000 persons over three days! Frank was a regular speaker along with Ned Meharg and others who were always ready to help with the ministry. Gene Train, Mark Mattix and the local brethren were glad to receive outside help with the teaching of the Word.)*

*Chapter 29*

# A SOJOURN ABROAD

The years 1962 to 1964 were very busy and eventful. There was much activity in evangelistic outreach in the city of Santa Cruz and nearby areas. Teams of helpers arrived and we all participated in seeking to reach people with the Gospel. The 1960 version of the Reina Valera had just been released to much fanfare. (The Reina Valera is the Spanish translation of the Bible, first done in 1569. It is the equivalent of the King James Version.)

We had "La Biblia para cada hogar" (The Bible in Every Home) team. Later this was followed by the "Pocket Testament League". Accompanying these efforts, the evangelical groups helped campaigns in the public stadium. There was prayerful support and a good relationship between the groups. There was also a large follow up work. It was a time of great excitement!

There was even a new openness by many who had opposed Bible reading and teachings before. The occurrence of the Second Vatican Council (1962-65) both reflected and augured an important shift in the relationship of the Roman Catholic Church with other Christian denominations. Spanish rather than Latin was used for the Mass, and Bible-reading was encouraged as the foundation of all Christian life and teaching. It brought an open mindedness among those who had been under the Roman Catholic doctrine. There was freedom to speak about and to read the Bible everywhere.

At the same time at the beginning of the 1960s, there was a definite distrust and rejection toward missionaries. In response to the repressive measures used by the government that had brought in the 1952 Revolutions (Chapter 7), an opposition party attempted a coup d'état in 1959. The brutal reaction to the failed attempt created an atmosphere of tension and rumour. One thing that both sides agreed on was that the presence of foreign missionaries was an affront. One heard about "black lists" and other damaging rumours were circulating. The Gospel campaigns mentioned above helped to ease the oppressive feeling of that time, but the political tension and underground resistance was mounting.

At Tambo Missionary School word came that the children had to pack a little bag and have it ready for escape in case of danger. Frank felt we should take our children out of the country. His worry was that the opposition could exile him but hold the Bolivian mother and children in the country. It was arranged that I would travel to Scotland with our four children. Frank would stay behind to stabilize work in the church and in the rural areas. He would join us later.

I and the four children started plans for the trip to Scotland. We were heading for Buenos Aires, Argentina, to catch the boat that would take us to the British Isles. Personally, I felt sure I could do everything by myself. It was the time when God had to teach me very clearly the necessity of depending on His guidance for every step of the way.

The children and I flew from Santa Cruz to Salta in Argentina. We had planned to make the rest of the trip by bus to Buenos Aires, rather a long journey, but we had not enough money to travel by air all the way. I carried with me two letters to deliver to folks in the city of Salta. Arriving in Salta we took a taxi to my sister Julia's house, where I was hoping to stay. On arrival I was told she was away with her husband.

Then I asked the driver to take us to the next address to deliver the second letter to a missionary couple. On arriving there, an older gentleman told me they were away but he did take the letter. As we walked back to the street, I asked him if he could direct me to a place to stay for the night, perhaps a Bed and Breakfast before we continued to Buenos Aires. He was a little flustered thinking I was asking for hospitality (something that happens to missionaries, and something I frankly would have appreciated but was too proud to ask!).

In the taxi the children were chattering in English among themselves while waiting on my return. Surprised by the children's use of the language, he asked me, "Who are these children?" I answered, "They are mine." Then he asked "Who are you?" I had to answer and lost my planned anonymity with which I had thought to help keep us out of trouble!

Following that, he offered his very kind hospitality and help in every possible way. The missionary couple returned later and received their letter which also mentioned me and my purpose in travelling. I hadn't realized how wrong I was in thinking I could manage the long trip on my own. Our Heavenly Father was determined to teach a lesson to a hard-headed woman!

And how I needed His and others' help during that trip! Here's just some of the things that happened:

I had brought some Money Orders to change in Argentina, but discovered there was a ban on them among the money changers unless a known local person was with me. Help! I had thought that booking bus tickets would be easy. Wrong! A local missionary had to do our booking and managed to advise other fellow missionaries of our passing through until we reached Buenos Aires. On arrival I was delighted to be met by a Scottish friend who took us to a home where I met a lovely Scottish missionary lady, Mrs. Wain, who was travelling on the same boat we were booked in. She was in second class, we were in third class. She loved bringing treats to the children from her dining room! We were together all the way to Glasgow, where she parted from us to go home to Edinburgh. What a delightful gift of friendship and fellowship enjoyed all the way.

(*My independent spirit had decided: "I can do it all by myself." God said: "You need to learn to be guided by Me and learn from Me."*

*Our Omniscient God knows every step of our way and wants us to look to Him for guidance. He desires that His children learn to discern His will and follow His leading, so we can serve Him better. By doing His will, we will find our life easier and happier even through difficult times.*)

Once in Scotland we were granted the use of the missionary apartment at Anniesland Cross in Glasgow. The children attended the nearest school in the Broomhill area, and walked to school every day accompanied by two neighbourhood children, Billy and Dorothy Jackson, who lived in the same building.

A few months later, Frank was able to join the family, stopping first in Miami, Florida, where he became acquainted with some believers in that city, and his ministry of teaching was greatly appreciated. Air travel was replacing the long sea journey. Money-wise it was much the same, but time-wise...! He flew from Miami to Glasgow Airport and in just a few hours joined the family in Glasgow. We were very happy to have him back with us.

After a busy and largely happy time in Scotland (and a couple of delightful months in Belfast visiting the Gilpins) soon it was time to think of our return to the field. Frank had received invitations to return via the United States, and he was granted an American visa which allowed him to speak in churches and receive help toward expenses.

We flew to New York, where we were met by good friends. It was our introduction to the American way of life. Soon we were on our way to Miami, Florida. We planned to stay only a few weeks on American soil. The plan was to buy a vehicle suitable for the work in Bolivia of visiting groups of believers in different areas. But there, the Lord stopped us for a period of time.

At that time (1966) Miami was absorbing many Cuban refugees who were fleeing from the Castro regime in search of peace and freedom. It was desperate for them as they were allowed only a change of clothing and a wedding ring as they boarded the airplanes of the Flights of Mercy the U.S. provided. They had to transfer all their belongings and assets to the Castro regime before being allowed to leave Cuba as exiles to the United States, Mexico or Spain. They arrived in Miami as paupers.

A group of believers in Bible Truth Chapel in downtown Miami generously opened the back hall of their chapel as a space for Cuban believers to meet, but they had no Spanish speakers. A Canadian missionary couple, Ralph and Marian Carter, moved from the Dominican Republic to work among the Cuban refugees who were like lost sheep after leaving everything they owned behind.

The Carters invited us to their home for a meal. They explained the nature of their activities. Then they asked if we could replace them for a few months to allow them to go home to Vancouver. We could stay in their home during their absence, and also use one of the cars parked on their patio. There was an elementary school within walking distance for the children.

After a time of waiting in prayer, we accepted the invitation. Frank still had things to do in the U.S. So, we moved into the Carters' house and they left, driving toward Vancouver. It was a long drive of more than six days. As they reached Washington State, close to home, Marian noticed that Ralph kept veering to the left. Something was wrong. After visiting a doctor, it was found that Ralph had a tumour in the brain. He died soon after they arrived home.

The sad news reached us. We had to make a new decision. Do we go? Do we stay? The new group of Cuban believers needed more grounding in the Scriptures before a group of elders would be ready to assume care of the assembly. The decision was taken to remain. Our children were accepted into the elementary school and we started our work with the dear Cuban folks. (We also experienced our first hurricane!)

Frank was busy teaching at Bible Truth Chapel and preaching in other places as well. I taught the little children in Spanish Sunday School until they reached school age, then they moved to the English group. Visitation was an important ministry since many of the refugees were homesick and lonely settling down in a new country.

Finally, Frank managed to find the vehicle he was looking for to take to Bolivia, a Camper truck. It was time to think about our return to Bolivia. However, one night as we were returning home in the Camper from the monthly missionary meeting, we met with an accident. As we were waiting at an intersection for a left turn, a car crashed into the back of our vehicle tearing out the rear of the camper truck. The two men in the car were clearly under the influence of alcohol. But when we went to the police station, Frank was charged! It was most unfair.

Finally, we had to go before the judge for sentencing. A lawyer friend was with us to help with the difficult situation. The judge, aware of the unfairness, introduced himself by saying: "Twenty years ago, I came to this country as an immigrant from Poland. This country has been kind to me and my family. Today we have a stranger in our midst. I feel that to honour what the U.S. has done for me, I need to give the following verdict: Mr. Haggerty, you have a suspended sentence!"

Frank turned horrified to his lawyer friend, only to find a big smile on the lawyer's face. He then explained that it meant Frank was free from all charges. Frank's immediate thought when he heard the word 'suspended sentence' was the image of the companion of his youth, John Grey, who finished suspended by the neck in Barlinnie prison!

At the same time as we prepared for our return to Bolivia, it seemed as though our activities in the U.S. intensified. Our children did well in school. The Spanish group was growing by leaps and bounds. Frank's ministry of sound solid teaching of the Word led to extended invitations (including a delightful sojourn in the Bahamas, while we renewed our U.S. visas).

(*During that time, Frank received an invitation from his friend Will Wilding (son of the Mr. Wilding in Scotland, Chapter 5). He invited Frank to come to Vancouver as the speaker at the Labour Day Camp for College and Careers. Frank had a wonderful time in Vancouver, found old friends from Scotland and Ireland, and made new ones.*

*God was preparing the way for decisions to be made in coming years for the family. We, the parents, had no idea that seven years later we would be heading for Vancouver, B.C., Canada for the higher education of our children. Nor that we would be able to take advantage of a temporary dispensation to immigrate once we were on Canadian soil in 1973. Nor that we would eventually become Canadian citizens and become deeply connected to the community of believers in Vancouver.*)

The time came for returning to Bolivia. After further teaching and fervent prayer, the two most responsible brethren in the Spanish group, Alfredo Magluta and Ramon Estevez, were named as elders and commended to the Lord for their future work in the church. We were happy to see the development of the work started by Ralph and Marian Carter.

(*Both Alfredo and Ramon continued faithfully. The work continued to develop well among the Spanish-speaking folks. More people were saved. Other Spanish speakers were also attracted.*

*However, the English group was dwindling. Many English-speaking people moved out of the area that had become known as Little Havana. Soon the English group started to look for property in a more English-speaking area, eventually moving to new premises in S.W. 99th Avenue, Miami, where they have done very well. They offered the 7th Street property to the Cuban folks, and stood by them as they negotiated the legal matters of the transfer of the property. Thus, the Iglesia Evangelica Calle Siete became established, and has continued to grow.)*

We finally returned to Bolivia with the satisfaction of knowing that our sojourn in American soil had brought fruit to the Glory of God. The deep friendship with our Cuban friends continued over the years. Seeing families grow and become part of the fellowship together with new arrivals from Cuba has been encouraging. We also left with a Camper that would allow us to continue our work of visitation and support to believers in the country areas of Bolivia.

Mr. F. J. Haggerty and his wife live in this coach as they seek to visit outlying assemblies in Bolivia. A difficult way of life, but a fruitful ministry.

*Chapter 30*

# CHURCH BUILDER

It has been mentioned earlier (Chapter 7) that as part of the Agrarian Reform, the Government offered land to people who were willing to go and settle down in the virgin lands of Santa Cruz province. Many Quechua accepted the challenge and moved down from the Andean mountains to the lowlands. They received a sizable piece of land that had to be cleared of trees before the land could be ready for agriculture. They began by clearing an area, each family working to build a shack for habitation.

They had no idea of the problems they would face in terms of mosquitos, bugs of all kinds, snakes, the tropical heat, and so on. It was terribly hard for them. Some were not able to settle due to the climate and the other challenges but many were determined to succeed in spite of the hard work that was required.

Some believers known to us from our time in the Andean region took advantage of the offer in order to better themselves, but also felt the challenge to go and preach the Gospel to other settlers. One of the early settlers, Angel Apala, was a faithful believer from the Altiplano, who claimed a portion of land, worked as needed and mostly became a missionary among the settlers preaching and teaching the Word of God. Unfortunately, the enemy used a poisonous snake to cut his life and ministry short.

Frank took up the challenge of working for the Lord in that district. He already knew some of the believers from our time in the Andean Altiplano. Although our base was in the city of Santa Cruz, we went and visited the different areas, encouraging the people. (Frank was the first missionary to move in among the settlers. Later other missionaries, such as Noel McKernon of New Zealand and Jim Neilson of Scotland joined forces in the outreach. Jim came when the McKernons went home on furlough.)

The settlers were having a tough time in their new lands, but everybody was spiritually tender. For the first time they were away, free from the patriarchal systems and authority of their Quechua elders. They were free to think and choose. But there was a spiritual void which led them to search for the truth. It was a time of great blessing. People were saved and baptized. In a number of settlements, small assemblies were started. The believers themselves witnessed to their new faith, and the Gospel news spread around like wild fire.

Yes, there was a great need of solid Bible teaching. We moved in there for extended periods with our Camper truck which housed us. (Our children had returned to the missionary boarding schools during the school year, which made it possible for us to be away from the city for longer periods.) Frank would give the teaching. We found it was necessary to give the study notes, so I would do the typing and printing, and before the next session they had the lessons printed and ready to take home for future reference. Just as he had done in Miami, Frank was becoming a Bible teacher and church builder, nurturing the small assemblies in the area.

Frank's training as a woodworker also enabled him to 'build churches' physically. He designed a sort of prefabricated hall made of wood panels that could be bolted together and sat on a proper foundation. The little hall could sit up to fifty persons. It gave the believers a place to meet and was a significant presence in the community to attract others.

When the believers felt the need of something bigger, they built a permanent metal frame on top of the wooden prefab, on a new and larger foundation. As the building was completed, the wooden prefab was disassembled and moved to another site that needed a building.

(*Who could have guessed that Frank's days in a work camp as a Conscientious Objector building prefabs would inspire his work as a literal church builder 30 years later! He used tropical hardwoods that were tough as nails (literally). The wooden prefab was good as a temporary building. It incentivised a new permanent building because it was so hot in the tropical sun! As I write this, that little wooden prefab building has been used to start seven different assembly gatherings.*)

But where there is blessing, the enemy of our souls is watching and ready to throw a spanner in the works.

*Conference Tujtapari*

Some people from the North of Argentina came to visit the settlers. Unfortunately, they were extremely legalistic and managed to capture those new believers to their teaching. It was a wave that flooded through the new Quechua believers, catching them in their new faith at a time when they had little knowledge of the Word but were very zealous.

Many Quechua believers pressed Frank to move with them and their ideas, but he would not go against his conviction as he saw it from the Word. Eventually folks turned against the missionaries, and especially against Frank. In fact, they officially excommunicated him, no longer receiving him as a brother. He had to abandon the work with the settlers with a broken heart. He had poured his life into teaching the believers and now they turned bitterly against him on secondary issues.

(*These things come and sift the church and also cause much heartache. It caused a major division which lasted for several years. After several years the divisive element withdrew, and many dear believers realized their mistake and apologized to Frank for the hurt that had been caused.*)

But for us, it was a signal that it was time to turn our eyes fully to the city-based work.

During those years both the city of Santa Cruz and the work were growing, but there was only one place for meetings, right in the heart of the city. There was a need to open assemblies in other areas of the growing city.

The important thing was to find a place where people were already living and start with a place that was big enough to hold a group of children. This could be in homes, patios or even under the shade of trees. Soon it resulted in parents becoming interested in the activities, and finally several of them would make a profession of faith in Christ. Other adults would become interested, and finally it became an assembly.

Most often this started in the home of a particular family. For instance, the work in the Lazareto area, started as a Children's Hour in the home of the Porcels, the family of Maria, sower of the seed (Chapter 19). My sister Mery and her husband, Heberto Ribera, gave themselves completely to the work in the new area, visiting, inviting and establishing friendships in the neighbourhood along with the Porcel family. As they outgrew the premises a site was bought in the vicinity and Frank built a large single-roomed structure, which was simple but adequate at the time. And a full-fledged assembly was soon started. Both the assembly and its building grew. In time, the original site was too small in Lazareto, and the elders decided that three elders would stay in the original assembly and three move out to a new area on the East side of the city where several people lived.

They purchased land. Frank worked with the men to build a room large enough to start. Seats were put in and the children's work was moved into it. Neighbourhood adults began showing interest and came. Very soon the assembly was established and the time came to hive off and move into other areas to start children's work and a new assembly. Several places started in this way in the city and later they began to reach out beyond the city limits.

The believers themselves realized they could do missionary work with their neighbours. Given the importance of the children's work in starting new assemblies, training in child evangelism group was very important. A German missionary lady, Petra Krikau, came into our assembly fellowship, and she was a great help in training our young people as tutors, and giving them the vision to work with children and to train others.

Sometimes land was purchased first, and some basic structures built or Frank put up his little wooden prefab and built a room to house a young couple. A place to stay was a great gift to some of our leading couples like Erasmo and Mercy, Juan and Diony, Geraldo and Eunice. Within a short time, they had a big group of children who were then followed by adults.

Land for these projects came about in a variety of ways. A Japanese believer donated a piece of land for a meeting place, that became Avenida Alemana Chapel. One believer in an area called Samaria lost his wife to cancer and donated his house to start an assembly. Those Samaritans have become very active in their testimony!

One purchase came about through frustration and then miraculous resolution that happened to us. The Postal Service in Bolivia was (still is!) poor and unreliable. Our bank in the U.S. decided to send cheque books to us by the post. One of these fell into bad hands and the person started to write cheques enjoying the ill-gotten gains. When we discovered the fraud, there was nothing we could do to find the thief, but Frank was in the States for a conference and went to visit the bank. They disclaimed all responsibility, even when Frank asked them to compare the signature of the signee against the filed signatures lodged in the bank. Frank returned to Bolivia quite disheartened. The loss was around $5000.00.

A few days after Frank's return to Bolivia, a group of believers from a new suburb came and begged Frank to help them to buy a corner property next to the hut where they were gathering. He told them that he didn't have any means to help because all the money had been cleaned out of the bank, but nonetheless he promised to help as much as possible.

Not long after, in our mailbox at the Post Office there was a letter from the Bank apologizing and explaining they had decided to make good all the money stolen! The bank balance was restored. ("Thank You, Lord, for this great intervention.") Frank called the brethren with the good news that they could go ahead with buying the land. They erected a fine building which has enabled them to gather a good number of people under the sound of the Gospel. Our God is a God of most incredible solutions!

(*Frank loved the challenge of designing small halls and building that made the best use of the space for assemblies. Our house was filled with sketches and architectural models of these buildings! But his talent as a carpenter and house builder was not the only way he helped build churches. Gradually, Frank's work and evident gifting shifted toward Bible teaching, especially to "equip the saints for the work of the ministry, for building up the body of Christ", Ephesians 4:12. Thus he became a church builder, in the much larger sense. Again, the house is filled with Frank's notes for messages and series on things like: The Holy Spirit; The Christian Home; A Doctrine of Man; and so on.*)

While many new assemblies were being built, we needed to take a hard look our place of meeting, the original hall ("Local Evangélico") in Calle Independencia. The central location made it easy to travel by public transport from most areas of the city.

The place was packed to overflowing on Sundays, with some standing right through the services. The building had undergone several enlarging projects, but it was now impossible to find more space. It was clearly time to think of a larger building.

The responsible brethren presented the idea to the congregation and a decision was made to look for property within the central area of the city. Everyone agreed together to start digging into pockets toward the project! An early plan was to use the money spent on the usual Coke to buy a brick for the new building! People were happy with this idea, "We can always drink water to quench our thirst!"

We discovered two properties selling side by side. Frank settled immediately on the smaller one, 15 metres front by 120 metres deep. When we returned to make an offer, after making sure there were sufficient funds to buy it, we discovered to our dismay that the larger property beside it been sold the day before to a Korean pastor who intended to build for their group.

By law in Bolivia, two churches cannot be built side by side. The Korean pastor agreed that he would offer Frank his property if the funds did not come in to cover the money he had borrowed. Several weeks later, the pastor called Frank to tell him that nothing was coming in to repay the loan and the lender was already demanding his money back. He offered the property as agreed, and we were ready to take it. That is how the larger property, 30 metres by 120 metres deep was acquired within the city area.

Frank went to his drawing board and presented a variety of designs. The final decision was for a building that seated over 900 persons, with room for more in the mezzanine gallery. "Big ideas for a small congregation", some jeered, but the congregation was on fire to gather the funds for the new building. Frank not only worked at the drawing board, but also worked physically alongside the builders.

(*The financing of the new building was based on the sale of property on Calle Independencia, which was valuable because of its central location. But a small dissenting group opposed the sale, and Frank in particular. This created a painful division as well as the financial hardship of having to bear the full weight of the new building. Frank was able to secure a loan of $100,000 from the Stewards Foundation. As guarantors of the loan we were responsible for repaying the 10-year loan according to the payment schedule - whether funds from the assembly were there or not! This was a stressful period for us, as it took the assembly almost 15 years to accumulate the total amount to repay the loan. It was a time of dependence on the Lord's provision and also drawing on the penny-pinching lessons of our early lean years! It became a wonderful opportunity for me to deepen relationships with the women in the assembly by working together on a variety of fund-raising initiatives like making and selling jams and baked goods and various crafts.*

*This time was also interspersed with a time of travel to Canada for health reasons for both Frank and me. I had a revision of an earlier hip replacement, as well as work done on my failing knees. Frank was having back problems and increasingly frequent angina pectoris.*)

Eventually, the building was ready, and opened officially in 1999 as Ebenezer - "Thus far the LORD has helped us" (1 Samuel 7: 12). On our return from Canada as the 21st Century started, the congregation held a special time of prayer and thanksgiving for the new building and for the 50 years of Frank's missionary service in Bolivia.

*(The new building was Frank's last project. It is a large, attractive building, and the large property has space for many different activities, including a basketball court. The building that seemed overly ambitious in 1999 has been well suited as members keep increasing, and the place is full on Sundays. The mezzanine gallery hosts a Bible Training Institute under the direction of Carlos ("Chaly") Aparicio; the Institute is open to all believers across the city who desire to study the Bible in a systematic way. Chaly is originally from Uyuni and became very much our son in the Lord. He has followed in Frank's footsteps as a good Bible teacher, and his wonderful wife Karina - one of my star Sunday School students - gradually assumed most of my roles with women's ministry and retreats.*

*In April 2019, Ebenezer celebrated the 20th year anniversary of the building. Frank would have been thrilled to see the approximately 400 people at the Breaking of Bread (that day there were many from surrounding assemblies, adding to the normal attendance of 100-150). The assembly is engaged in two church plants on the outskirts of the city.)*

*Chapter 31*

# BIG CHANGES

During the 1960s and 70s, Bolivia started to come out of the "dark ages" in many ways. The Reforms mentioned earlier (Chapter 7) had brought many positive changes. Schools were functioning even in the remotest places. There was now freedom to read the Bible, and greater availability in Indigenous languages and dialects through the efforts of New Tribes Mission working together with the Wycliffe Bible Translators.

The migration of people to the lowlands as part of the Agrarian reform enabled people to own land and produce abundant crops. So different from the hard toil of the Andean Plateau. As people were converted they began to change their lifestyle and many showed by the way they now lived what the influence of Bible teaching and faith in Christ had done for their lives and families.

For many years the province of Santa Cruz had been neglected by the government. But City of Santa Cruz authorities took their development into their own hands. They started cooperatives to provide electric, water and telephone services, enlisting every home to participate in the initiative. In this way they provided stable energy supplies, safe water, telephone and other services. This supported incredible growth and the city started to expand.

*(From the small city of 50,000 that Frank encountered when he arrived in 1951, it is now a modern city with a population of close to 2 million and it extends in size more and more. It is the economic engine of Bolivia.)*

At the mid-1970s and 80s as our work changed from visiting and supporting the many assemblies of settlers in the country areas, a completely unexpected opportunity arose for home Bible studies among upper class Roman Catholic women. In the wake of the Second Vatican Council, a charismatic movement and spiritual awakening took place in Latin America. As Roman Catholics began reading the Bible, they experienced a great thirst for teaching and some perplexity as they could not find in the Scriptures many of the things they had believed were scriptural truth, like St. Anne being the mother of Mary, or the Virgin Mary's assumption.

Women from some of the leading families in Santa Cruz came to Frank and me to ask for Bible lessons. This was so different from the attitude of rejection of the Gospel message suffered earlier by pioneer believers. It was so different from the social ostracism that I experienced when my mother and I declared ourselves to be evangelical believers. The ostracism extended to the whole of family, as 'non-conformists'.

But they again recognized me as one of their own, and with a valuable asset! They could not bring themselves to darken the door of a "Local Evangélico", but they opened their hearts and homes to read the Bible and hear the Gospel. After a few years, the two charismatic priests who supported their spiritual and Scriptural quest were moved on to other parishes where they would cause less trouble. But the flood gates had been opened, and it became much more common to be a Gospel-believing Spirit-filled Christian regardless of the denomination.

*(Now when a person says and shows he or she is a true believer, they are accepted and trusted as honest, God-fearing people. It is almost a mark of honour to be an evangelical believer! However, having said this, there has been proliferation of sects and cultic preachers who seek to attract people away to themselves. Sadly there are always wolves dressed as sheep in the gatherings, but "by their fruits, ye shall know them".)*

One night in 1978, Frank was returning home on a motorbike. (The pick-up truck had been borrowed to take the young people home.) A vehicle collided with Frank and he was left unconscious in the street. The accident was witnessed by two young men who recognized Frank and knew where he lived. They very kindly brought Frank home and left. I was quite upset but thanked the young men and went inside to look after Frank. In my haste I neglected to ask them details about the incident.

Frank must have had severe concussion. He also sustained a broken shoulder which had to be attended to. He could not remember what took place and did not know who and where he was. A doctor came and we made Frank comfortable for the night. The next day Frank asked where he was and why he was in a strange place. His memory took him back to Scotland. He didn't know he had a wife and family! However, in time things started coming to him slowly. I was truly thankful. But Frank never remembered the details of the accident, even though we went to the very scene. It was wiped out of his memory to the end of his days.

This accident caused Frank to have to lie low for a while. This he found very hard. But the accident changed things. Long after his shoulder had mended, and he looked well, he felt fragile. He tired easily. Many years later, he would attribute the beginning of difficulty with memory to this incident.

*Frank Haggerty*

The Lord changed Frank's sphere of ministry in his latter years. While he continued his labours in Santa Cruz, especially teaching, the brethren in the assembly were increasingly able to take on the work. This allowed Frank freedom to accept invitations to teach and preach in Argentina, the U.S. and Canada. The elders in Santa Cruz kept the difficult problems to discuss with Frank at his return which allowed them to grow as elders in the assembly and develop their experience and wisdom.

The Argentinian believers especially enjoyed his teaching at conferences and special meetings. Often teaching is better received from a visitor. In one assembly, Frank went to the evening meeting almost immediately after he had arrived. He started giving his teaching as had been agreed. As the session progressed, someone in the audience stood up and blurted, "Who told you all that?" Surprised by the sharp question, Frank said, "What do you mean?" Other voices joined in and it became a free for all, with accusations flying around. Frank begged for silence and then asked for an explanation. It turned out that the members had been arguing fiercely with one another about certain Biblical issues which were dividing the fellowship. They were at their wits' end and when they heard the visiting speaker address the sore points, they felt sure someone from one side must have spoken to Frank about it. As things became more peaceful, Frank realized he had been specifically directed by the Holy Spirit to touch the very issues causing the dissension. That night the gathering continued till after 2.00 am, when everybody was able to appreciate and accept the teaching of the Word. Finally, they all apologized to one another and fellowship and peace were restored.

The Lord had sent a stranger to them. Under the Holy Spirit's leading, though ignorant of the problems in their midst, Frank was used to help the believers to resolve their differences.

An amusing incident happing in 1982 during the conflict between Argentina and Great Britain over the Falkland Islands (Islas Malvinas). Frank happened to be in Argentina as the main speaker at a large conference. Apparently word had gotten around of the "visiting English speaker" and when this word got to the ears of the police force, they sent a platoon of soldiers to arrest "Frank Haggerty, the British spy". They took him to the police station and started interrogating him about his "spying" activities. Poor Frank was really confused. Finally, he produced his Canadian passport, and a group from the assembly arrived to verify the fact that he was the speaker invited from Bolivia. Eventually he was allowed to continue his activities!

*(But these teaching activities also took a tremendous toll on Frank. He never took the responsibility of teaching lightly and spent many days in preparation. His time away was always very intense, with many additional sessions giving individual pastoring and advice. Despite appearances, Frank was actually quite introverted, and he found the intense social activity taxing.*

*He would return home absolutely drained. I had to learn to let him rest for several days before even trying to get a word out of him. And then I needed to clear my time to be able to listen, as he poured out all that had happened.*

*Frank continued his teaching and travelling for many years. But gradually he began to experience more and more difficulty with his memory. He had always been able to draw on the deep well of his intimate knowledge of the Scriptures, easily quoting passages and connecting the most obscure references by chapter and verse. He was terrified at finding himself lost at times in the middle of a message, and he had to prepare his messages almost word for word. After speaking at a 1993 Uplook Ministries Conference, Frank made the painful decision that he could no longer preach publicly.*

*Thanks to the invitation of a sensitive brother at the 16th Avenue Chapel in Vancouver, Frank found a new freedom in the ministry of prayer. And in visiting people in the hospital of all things - precisely the one activity he always had avoided! In prayer there was no searching for lost words, just speaking simply to his Beloved Lord and Saviour on behalf of someone else.)*

*Afterword*

# FRANK HAGGERTY, THE MAN

In Isaiah 51:1 God tells His people: *"Look to the rock from which you were cut out, to the quarry from which you were hewn"*.

Frank Haggerty never forgot where he came from. He never forgot the radical changes that took place after he met his Saviour, Jesus Christ. He remembered how one of the teachers at St. Peter's School, fed up with him and his unpleasant pranks, yelled at him, "You are going to finish in the gallows, Haggerty!" He could have lived the life of his friend John Grey who ended his life on the gallows. Yes, it might have happened but for the persistent witness of a faithful man, Harry Burness. He testified to God's grace and to His power to change even a young gang leader. Harry coupled his witness with hospitality. He began by sharing a piece of pie out of his lunch box, then invited the young hoodlum to his home for a good Scottish tea. Harry never knew that the first time Frank went to his home, the newly-saved gang leader was 'casing the joint' to see how easily the home could be broken into. But already the Holy Spirit had planted a conviction of right and wrong behaviour within Frank who put the wrong thoughts out of his mind and started enjoying the friendship of the home that had been opened to him. It was a home that planted in his mind the dream of a home for himself and a family (God willing).

Not surprisingly hospitality was practised in our home from the beginning and it was a tremendous help in making new friends and introducing them to the Lord.

Frank was very fond of quoting a portion found in Psalm 113: 7, *"He lifteth up the poor out of the dust, the needy out of the dunghill"*. He was always humbly thankful for what the Lord and the Lord's people had done to change him. Verse 8 of Psalm 113 follows, *"That He may set him with princes, even with the princes of His people"*. Frank grew in Bible knowledge under the guidance of Harry Burness and the influence of the folks at Summerfield Hall. He had an insatiable thirst for the study of the Holy Scriptures, which led him to meet other like-minded people. In time he also developed good and clear discernment in the Scriptures, and became a good teacher of the same.

The deep knowledge of Scripture and ability to teach brought him into contact with other able and gifted students of Scripture. We could call them *'princes of His people'*. He was awed by being treated with respect and as a peer by Bible teachers whom he admired so deeply and who had formidable formal training in the Scriptures. Yet Frank never allowed thoughts of pride to fill his head. He knew it all came from the Lord.

But he was proud when he finished a good piece of woodwork. He never got over his love for the beautiful tropical hardwoods in Bolivia. He enjoyed others' craftsmanship and loved his time in the workshop. Seeing the finished article brought him pleasure.

The *'princes of His people'* at Summerfield Hall trained Frank in manners and speech as well as Scripture. On one occasion when in Glasgow, Frank was invited by his old friend, Dr. Jim McNeill, to give a report on the work in Bolivia to the church. He did his usual good presentation and at the end a retired school principal came to the friend and congratulated him for having brought such a fine gentleman to speak to the audience that night. On the way home all of us had a good laugh over the "gentleman's" pedigree from Partickbridge Street in Glasgow!

Another good trait that governed his life was the fact that he held true to his convictions based on his knowledge of Scripture, regardless of social pressure. He was offered positions and places that could mean a comfortable life, "if you come with us" from different levels of society. Even when it meant that he would be excluded from fellowship among the Quechua groups he had so invested in, or when the upper classes in Santa Cruz society wanted to enjoy his teaching but not his church, he was faithful to his convictions and behaved according to the truth he found in Scripture.

His sense of adventure was good for travelling, preaching and teaching and always meeting new people, despite being quite an introvert. His adventures on horseback figured large in his illustrations when preaching, long after he could no longer undertake the adventures in person.

Frank closed his missionary service well. Three years after opening the new church building, he went to be with the Lord on 4 October 2003 at the age of 78 years. His funeral attendance filled to overflowing, both inside and outside, the new building he had designed to seat 900. Many bore witness to his influence in their lives and to small and large acts of generosity (some that were news to me!). His was a life well-lived and well-used for his Saviour. He was buried in a small missionary mausoleum, next to Mr. Peter Horne.

*Frank & Blanquita Haggerty*

## FELLOW BOLIVIAN WORKERS REMEMBERED

In looking back there are some names of believers that have a sweet aroma surrounding them. Many men and women faithfully serve the Lord and His Church in many different parts of Bolivia, reaching out to the unsaved with the gospel of Salvation through faith in Christ. Some in full-time service.

From the Uyuni times I remember Crispin Huanca and his wife Maria, who were very faithful in their service for the Lord. Crispin was always ready to accompany Frank on many trips. After he bought his Bible and trusted the Lord, he started working on his sisters and families who came to hear the Word of Salvation. He also sought faithfully to bring up his family in the knowledge of the Lord. All of them eventually left Uyuni seeking further education for their children and were instrumental in consolidating the assembly work in Cochabamba and other places. Ultimately, the family moved to Santa Cruz where they have continued their good testimony.

Enrique Bazan was a rough individual who, after coming to faith in Christ, discovered he had a gift to sell Scriptures and became the best colporteur in Bolivia, selling Bibles to all and sundry.

From our time spent in Alkatuyo, we remember Pablo Mamani, the Quechua aristocrat, who was a great helper in the work in the country areas of Potosi. Pablo moved down to the lowlands taking advantage of the Government offer of free land. He worked on the land but he also worked tirelessly in spreading the Gospel message among the settlers. Often he moved to a different area to work the land, but mainly to preach the Word. He was a frequent visitor to our home in Santa Cruz seeking tracts, Bibles, booklets or any other materials to help with the outreach of the Gospel.

Many outstanding believers have been raised from and around Santa Cruz. Roberto Filtrin came to Santa Cruz from Puerto Suarez. Frank became his mentor. Eventually he spoke to Frank about his desire to give himself full time to help in the assembly. Roberto became an elder in the assembly and became a true shepherd. There was no opportunity missed to spread the Gospel whether it be jails, hospitals, open airs, or further afield.

Eliseo Zuñiga, from La Paz, has been a true servant who has given himself to the Lord's Work, both in the written and spoken ministry, faithfully visiting assemblies around the country.

Similarly, my sister Mery and her husband Heberto Ribera gave themselves fully to the care of the new assembly in the Lazareto area, and extended their activities to other outreaches. Now like many of the others feeling the passage of time, they are quietly looking forward to the coming of their Lord.

The Great Comission was given to the disciples after the Resurrection and repeated again at the Ascension in Acts 1 verse 8, *"You shall be witnesses unto Me both in Jerusalem, and in all Judaea and in Samaria, and unto the uttermost part of the earth".* It emboldened the disciples to preach the Gospel. Persecution caused them to start moving further out reaching souls for God. Many were martyred, but many have been reached and lives changed by the transforming power of the Holy Spirit.

**Blanquita Haggerty, 2018**

*Epilogue*

# FRANK & BLANQUITA REMEMBERED

What a gift to have this story of the life and work of Frank and Blanquita Haggerty, our parents. We knew our parents were not like other missionaries nor like our uncles and aunts, and sometimes that was uncomfortable. As the children of Blanquita and Frank Haggerty, we lived this long life with them. We grew up with strong and remarkable parents, undertaking exciting journeys that felt like a reliving of the book of Acts.

We also watched the heavy toll of that life on them as they aged, and eventually, as they passed. Several years before he died, Dad confessed that, as he was pouring out his complaint to the Lord about how his heart and body had been broken in the service of God's people, he received a correction and gentle reminder: he had not been called to be the servant of the Lord's people but of the Lord Himself. This realization gave him a new freedom and a return to his first love.

The reality of the missionary life is that it is hard. It requires stepping out of the usual stream of human activity, following the road less travelled. This calling began with our parents, but the challenges extended outwards, to family, to close friends, to those whom the calling has affected. This challenge was also met, not in the least, by those who generously gave to this great commission. It is the pebble of a missionary life thrown into the deep pool of the human condition, and which continues to make waves long after the pebble disappears.

Looking back, we realise how truly remarkable our parents were. Mum has provided a detailed portrait of Dad, but she has been shy about speaking of herself and her own achievement. We are not.

Mum mentions her regret at not being able to pursue her schooling when she was needed to look after her siblings and distressed mother after the family fire (Chapter 18). She does not let on that she only had three years of formal education that was interrupted by her arthritic episodes. This lacunae that she felt so deeply was never evident to us or others. Mum's trip abroad to Brazil when she was 19 years old cemented in her a deep love of language, and from that time forward, Mum always spoke an impeccable and international Spanish. She insisted on the same for her children, and she and we were/are often teased about speaking like foreigners. In her later years she discovered her voice as a writer, and became a regular contributor to *Caminemos Juntas*, a Spanish magazine for Christian women. As she aged, Spanish became again her dominant language and where her real eloquence emerged.

But Mum established English as the language of the home so that we would be prepared for international travel and study. What discipline this took! Mum learned the language as we learned it, aided principally by her copy of the parallel English-

Spanish King James Bible. Dad - for whom the language of the Bible was normal - sometimes neglected to update Mum's English for the 20th Century, much to her consternation when went to Scotland in 1957! She kept learning: reading avidly and doing daily cross-word puzzles to hone her vocabulary. Her inimitable Scottish-Spanish-accented English was layered with expressions and pronunciation that reflected the time and space where she learned them. ("O, Ma-a-an!" she would exclaim with an ersatz American twine.)

Mum was also remarkable within the prevailing macho culture of Bolivia for insisting that her sons as well as daughter participate in house chores. She knew she was training us for study abroad and to live on our own. As she mentioned in the book, the Haggerty table was a place of hospitality, and Mum was a master of stretching food and pennies to feed many. She passed on to her spiritual daughters her inside knowledge of how to feed hundreds of hungry campers three meals a day for less than $1 each! She also passed to her children her secrets of cooking delicious but inexpensive meals. To this day, you are guaranteed a good meal at a Haggerty house!

Above all, Mum was a model of determination, perseverance and hard work. It could be exhausting to be around her! She was determined to keep active physically, not giving in to the pain of her arthritis even when it hurt. After she got her first hip replacement at the age of 46 years, her visible relaxation and ability to laugh easily was, for her teen-aged children, a startling revelation of the constant pain in which she had been functioning and an explanation of the steely determination. As she faded, she gauged her tiredness by standards of work - "I have just gotten off the airplane coming back from Canada" or "We just finished camp" or "It must be Christmas" and so on. In her final vulnerability, she accepted help readily, expressing sweet gratitude and amazement at the strength and determination of her helpers.

What a legacy!

Blanquita was Frank's helpmeet to the end. Dad built in 1971 a family home in Santa Cruz on Mum's inherited land in the city. This grounded Mum and Dad's work in a new way - so different from the early years of "pilgrimage" described in the book. The home also became a centre for us children as we began our own pilgrimages in the world pursuing our respective careers. Mum and Dad's insatiable appetite for learning allowed them to enjoy vicariously the respective university programs we pursued in Canada.

Canada also became the new sending country. As Dad and Mum needed more regular medical care, they began to divide their time between Canada and Bolivia. They were embraced by the Vancouver believers especially in Hollyburn, 16th Avenue and New Westminster. There, they enjoyed refreshment and rest from some of the challenges of their work in Bolivia.

As Dad lost his memory and his capacity to preach, it was Mum's ministry with women that took them back to Bolivia, including for his last year. The weight of details of his public work and obligations to people fell away, and he came "home" to his family and loved ones in his essential sweet self. In the end, he recognized love above all as Mum and other loved ones cared for him 24 hours a day. As he passed quietly into his Lord's loving presence, his last word was "Blanquita!".

After Dad's passing, Mum returned to splitting her time between Santa Cruz and Vancouver. In Santa Cruz, the Haggerty table of hospitality became the new centre for her ministry as she counselled women and mentored a selected group to take on her work organizing camps and retreats. Cohorts of her Sunday School "girls" - now in their 50s, 60s and 70s! - continued to visit her. Mum's own six-month retreats in Vancouver continued until 2018. After a knee replacement surgery that Mum recognized to be her final major medical intervention, she decided that it was time to move permanently back to Bolivia to be close to family and to where she still felt useful.

At the family home, a second storey had been built for Liam and his wife Miriam. They were close and always on hand to help. They were a critical support during the lockdown of the 2020 COVID-19 pandemic, especially as Mum was becoming more frail. By her 90th birthday in October 2020, Mum was fed up with the frailty of her mind and body, and especially frustrated by no longer being able to see well enough to read. When she was diagnosed with advanced liver cancer in December 2020, and she knew that, at last, she was being called home. Ian, Liam, Jeannie, granddaughter Fernanda and companion Rosa had the privilege of providing Mum's end-of-life care until she passed into the Lord's immediate presence on February 10th, 2021.

Like Frank, Blanquita closed her missionary service well. As the first commended Bolivian woman missionary in the Brethren assemblies, she opened a path for other women. She was a spiritual mother to many: not shy about pulling an occasional ear but mostly giving own her ear and heart to listen. At her funeral, many of her spiritual sons and daughters bore witness to her life and work. Hers was a life well-lived and well-used for her Saviour, her Lord and her people. She was buried in the small missionary mausoleum, with her beloved Frank. The epitaph she chose for him applied to them both: "having served [their] generation by the will of God, [they] fell asleep…" (Acts 13:36)

**Ian, Liam, Jeannie and Philip Haggerty, 2021**